D0296152

CAKES
from Concept to Creation

Dutton
PUBLISHING

PUBLISHING

First published in March 2002 by b. Dutton Publishing Limited, Alfred House, Hones Business Park, Farnham, Surrey, GU9 8BB.

Copyright: Kathy Moore 2002

ISBN: 0-9532588-3-1

All rights reserved.

No part of this publication may be reproduced, stored in a retrieval system or transmitted in any form or by any means electronic, mechanical, photocopying, recording, or otherwise, without prior written permission of the copyright owner. A catalogue record for this book is available from the British Library.

Kathy Moore has asserted her right under the Copyright, Designs and Patents Act, 1988, to be identified as the author of this work.

Publisher: Beverley Dutton

Editor: Jenny Stewart

Design: Sarah Richardson

Photography: Alister Thorpe

Printed in Spain

CONTENTS

FOREWORD

I started teaching over forty years ago in the art of cake design and other aspects of flour confectionery. One of the best aspects of this industry is that you meet many very talented people, both teachers and students. When I first had the pleasure of meeting Kathy I was amazed at her enthusiasm for cake artistry. Since then, I have seen her demonstrations and also taught alongside her.

Kathy is exceedingly talented in her profession and her incredible enthusiasm brushes off on all her students. Her work is always immaculate and her heartfelt passion to share her knowledge with others is an inspiration to any tutor or demonstrator.

When she first spoke to me about writing a book on cake making and design, I knew that, with her experience and brilliant teaching skills, Kathy would write a thoroughly informative and useful book. Cakes from Concept to Creation is an excellent source for both tutors and students alike - it guides the reader through every stage of the cake making and designing process, highlighting the potential pitfalls on the way and offering plenty of useful tips.

Eddie Spence MBE

Demonstrator, Judge and Lecturer of Cake Decoration and Design

This book is dedicated with the greatest love to my husband, Stephen.
Thank you for your endless love, patience, encouragement, help and fun!

"My God loves me,
His love will never end,
He lives within my heart,
For my God loves me."

Author unknown

INTRODUCTION

Cakes from Concept to Creation sets out - in logical sequence - the information a cake decorator needs to consider when planning to produce a high-standard, professional style wedding or celebration cake, no matter how simple or complex the overall design.

This is achieved by guiding you through the options available to you on such things as cake bases, shapes, sizes, tiers, types of icing, colour, and final presentation. It is intended that this book should be a feast of information not just on wedding and celebration cakes, but for other cakes, as information is provided on relevant quantities, portions, dowelling, display and presentation. Hopefully, therefore, this book will be of benefit not just to the new cake decorator, but also as a reference source to all involved in sugarcraft.

My introduction to professional cake decorating came many years ago, when I had promised to make a royal iced three-tier wedding cake for a dear friend. Three tiers, royal iced, 6", 9" and 12" round, with sugar flowers for all tiers and piped embroidery. It sounds very simple now, but as it was probably only my second wedding cake ever it was a prodigious task.

The challenge was set! Excitement, pleasure, anticipation and nerves became the norm over the next few weeks. My husband must have had the patience of a saint - cakes drying everywhere, tools and equipment all over the kitchen, sugar flowers in the dining room and on two occasions he even went to work with traces of lilac dusting powder on his usually pristine white, crisply starched collars!

But finally, the cake stood ready, pillar positions marked, flowers finished and arranged on the tops of each tier, and a tiny matching spray attached to the ribboned cake knife. I was delighted. It was Tuesday, the cake was to be delivered Wednesday evening and we were going away on Thursday.

The only thing remaining to do was to take the all-important photograph. I carefully positioned the pillars and erected each tier, then placed the knife beside the cake. How excited I was to see the finished cake, assembled on the dining room table, ready to be photographed, all the hard work behind me - or so I thought.

Camera in hand, I focused the lens, but I needed to be higher up to get the whole cake in the frame. I carefully balanced myself on an old stool and started to take the photograph. It looked wonderful! It was at this point that the stool started to wobble, I overbalanced and started to freefall towards the wedding cake! In seconds I saw the top tier decapitated from the middle; in mid-fall I tried frantically to grab it, hitting my chin on the table and landing in a none too elegant position on the floor. I had caught the top tier but, oh, what a mess the flowers were. Still, I knew I had spares so things did not look too bad after all - or so I thought.

I picked myself up off the floor and caught a glimpse of the other two tiers: I then realised I had serious problems. Miraculously the bottom tier had remained intact, but the middle tier looked very sick indeed. The flowers were broken and a large crack - emanating from the centre of the cake and continuing down the side - had appeared. Oh dear. Calming myself and rationalising, I knew all I had to do was replace the broken flowers and cover up the cracked icing. Things did not seem so bad - or so I thought.

I took the middle tier, covered the crack with royal icing as neatly as I could and then brought in an electric fan heater, put it on full power and left the icing to dry. Meanwhile, I went to replace the damaged flowers with the spares, knowing that all I had to do afterwards was complete the repair on the royal icing with some decorative piping. Things were looking up - or so I thought.

A short while later I returned and looked at the cake in horror - the heat from the fan heater had completely crazed the whole cake: it was cracked all over and resembled crazy paving! Be brave, I told myself, don't panic. I again rationalised - all I had to do was to take the royal icing off completely and re-ice - or so I thought.

I started to take the royal icing off, but the heat from the fan heater had melted the marzipan beneath! Be brave, I told myself, don't panic. I again rationalised - all I had to do was to take the marzipan off, re-cover and re-ice - or so I thought.

I started to take the marzipan off, only to find that the heat from the fan heater had turned the cake into a horribly soft and sticky mass - completely inedible! At this point, I was not very brave, nor did I want to rationalise. My confidence was completely shattered.

It was nearly lunchtime - I had one and a half days to do something. But what? I had no cake. I telephoned local shops but, no, they had no spare cake bases. I telephoned a friend: she was even more shocked than I was, saying she could not imagine what to do and if it was her she would feel like running away! I telephoned my Mum and as Mums always do, she said all the right things, calmed me down, talked things through and gave me the confidence to start all over again.

So, I put the oven on, jumped in the car, bought new supplies from the supermarket, mixed up the rich fruit cake, measured the brandy, put some in the cake and drank the rest. The cake was in the oven by 12.45pm and I started to mix up a new batch of royal icing. By 5.45pm the cake was out of the oven and cooling. It was going to be a late night. Thankfully it was winter and by midnight the cake was cold. I marzipanned it, cleared up, and half an hour later put the first layer of icing on the sides. An hour later, the first top coat went on, then it was left for what remained of the night.

The following morning the second layer went on and by lunchtime the third and final layer had been completed on both the top and sides. All that remained for me to do was add the decorative piping, dowel the cakes and secure the flowers to the top of the cake.

With decorations now complete and flowers secure, I had finally finished. I had my complete three-tier wedding cake sitting there before me with not even a hint of the disaster that had struck just eighteen hours before. How very lucky I had been. I still didn't have a photograph of the cake....and no, I didn't bother!

Although it had been very stressful, I learned so much from that single incident. Cake decorating is not just a case of 'not taking risks', but also demands a professional approach to the whole process. I vowed to myself to do it properly, to plan at the outset, to design before I had baked the cake, and to keep a proper record of how to do it.

Having refined the process over many years, demonstrated it and taught it - now is the time to share it with others in written form. So here it is, a book full of information to help you produce a wedding or celebration cake that will reflect the care and thought you have put in and of which you can be justifiably proud.

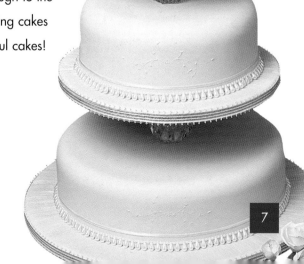

The chapters which follow start with the relevant information to assist you in making decisions on the cake before finalising your design, through to the production of a cake, and finish with advice on making and selling cakes from home. I hope this book helps you in your quest for successful cakes!

CAKE BASES

The bride and groom, parents, or the hosts of a celebration may all want to be involved in considering the various types of cake bases available and deciding which one (or combination) might suit them best. It may be intended that one tier of a wedding cake is to be kept for a subsequent celebration and therefore a cake base which will keep needs to be considered. They may want a cake that can also be served as a dessert, so a light sponge or chocolate cake base could be used. This chapter covers the principal options to consider, accompanied by a chart setting out timescales for baking, icing and keeping times (see page 127). Using this information, you should be able to choose a cake base or combination of bases that best suit your requirements and design.

TYPES OF CAKE BASES

RICH FRUIT CAKE

A cake termed 'rich' is one that contains a high proportion of fat to flour. As much as 350g/^{3}/$_4$lb to 450g/1lb of fat is used to 450g/1lb of flour before adding sugar, eggs and moist plump dried fruits. Often, the dried fruit content will be well over 55% of the whole cake content. It is the quantity and ratio of these ingredients that define a rich fruit cake, the richness also providing you with a cake of excellent keeping qualities. This is a traditional cake which can be made two to three

months ahead of time. During this period the fruits and sugars 'mature' giving improved flavour, richness and texture to the cake. Even cutting the cake will improve as the cake matures (cutting a newly made rich fruit cake may tend to be rather crumbly). Because of its weight, rich fruit cake provides an excellent stable base for sugarpaste or royal icing and is suitable for all decorative work.

This type of cake enables you to start well in advance and takes the stress out of last-minute baking and decorating: the decorative work can be completed one to two weeks ahead of time. Once the celebration is over, any cake not cut into will normally keep for up to a year if it is stored correctly, i.e. in a cool dry place away from any damp, humidity and direct sunlight. For factory produced cakes, refer to the manufacturer's instructions. Cakes should not be stored in plastic containers (which can cause the cakes to sweat and a mould may form), but in a strong cardboard box with a well-fitting lid (available from local bakers and sugarcraft shops).

SEMI-RICH FRUIT CAKE

This term refers to a less rich and lighter textured cake with a lesser quantity of dried fruit. This is a good alternative for those who are not fond of the traditional cake as it will still provide a good stable base for decoration and can be sugarpasted or royal iced. Once made, it will keep for a maximum of ten days (unless the recipe states differently), provided it is stored correctly. Semi-rich cakes can also be baked ahead of time and frozen.

MADEIRA CAKE

A good, moist, fairly close textured cake, usually without fruit. It is often used for one or more tiers in a wedding cake as an alternative to rich fruit because it is delightfully moist, can be flavoured, and because of its close texture, is firm enough to take both marzipan and sugarpaste (or other coverings). It is excellent for cutting and shaping, so is ideal for novelty cakes. It is an unsuitable base for royal icing as it is relatively light in comparison to a rich fruit or semi-rich fruit cake, and is more vulnerable to movement which could cause particularly fine or delicate work (for example, extension work and filigree work) to break or the icing itself to crack. Providing that the design is more substantial and the icing used is strong, lace work would generally be suitable.

I am often asked how far ahead Madeira cakes can be made. I always err on the side of caution and bake them just three days before needed. (A Madeira is often better textured after three days and cuts more easily.) This still gives plenty of time for decoration. The cake should be eaten within a further two to three days. Inevitably, because of the short timescale between baking and eating, there will be some last-minute work, so thought needs to be given to the design. With a well planned design, most of the decoration can be prepared in advance and placed onto the cake when iced, leaving minimal work (or something that is manageable within the timescale) on the actual cake. Madeira cakes can be made well ahead of the time required and frozen, but once thawed must not be re-frozen.

VICTORIA SANDWICH

This is made with a mixture containing equal quantities of butter, sugar, flour and egg. Victoria sandwich cakes should have a deliciously light, soft, moist and even texture when baked, less dense and less firm than that of a Madeira. They will take both marzipan and sugarpaste coverings - providing the combined weight is not too great for the cake - but are not suitable as royal iced cakes. A thin layer of buttercream is often used to attach sugarpaste (or any other rolled covering) to the cake. Victoria sandwich cakes are quick and easy to make and incredibly versatile with many variations available such as coffee, lemon, vanilla, almond, chocolate chip and walnut. They should be made only one or two days before required and eaten within a further two to three days, although they can be baked and frozen ahead of time. As with the Madeira, decorations can be prepared beforehand, ready to place onto the cake.

Care should be taken if splitting and filling cake bases as, if overfilled, or if the filling is very soft, it will bulge at the sides and a good, smooth, even sugarpasted (or other rolled covering) finish is difficult to achieve.

CHOCOLATE CAKE

Chocolate cakes are an increasingly popular choice for wedding or celebration cakes. There are many recipes, some of which result in a very light cake whilst others a finer and firmer close-textured cake, so it is important to ensure the recipe you are using is suitable for the decoration and design proposed. The weight of both marzipan and sugarpaste (both are available as chocolate flavoured, see Chapter 2 - Icings, Fillings and Decorative Pastes) may be too heavy for some recipes, so replacing the marzipan with a thin layer of good buttercream may be a better option. Alternatively, a recipe resulting in a good firm base, similar to a Madeira, poses no problem, and a high standard of finish is easily achievable. What may appear to be a traditionally decorated three-tier wedding cake could in fact be the cover for the most delicious of chocolate cakes!

A chocolate cake need not be a traditionally decorated style either, but could be filled with a rich and irresistibly moorish ganache filling, decorated with white chocolate caraque and hand-modelled chocolate roses. This would definitely need to be prepared and finished at the last moment, so it is essential to make sure you have everything to hand. Most chocolate cakes can be frozen ahead of time. Chocolate caraque can now be bought ready made in white, dark and milk chocolate to place directly onto the cake, and as the chocolate roses can be prepared at least a week in advance, this type of cake is becoming increasingly popular as it can also double up as a dessert. Remember that ganache is made with fresh cream so needs to be kept refrigerated. (See Favourite Recipes for instructions on making ganache.)

CROQUEMBOUCHE

A croquembouche is a traditional centrepiece for christenings, first communions and weddings in France. They are becoming increasingly popular as wedding cakes in the UK as they are not only a superb table centrepiece, but can also be served as a dessert.

A croquembouche is made up of many small filled profiteroles which, when baked, expand leaving an incredibly light outer pastry shell with a virtually hollow interior. The profiteroles are then filled with sweetened or flavoured cream and stuck together with a light caramel to form a large cone 60cm/24" or more high and placed on a nougatine base. A croquembouche is often decorated with praline, spun sugar and skilled boiled sugar work. However, it can be more easily decorated with sugar flowers, which makes it far more achievable and practical for most sugarcrafters and would make a beautiful table centrepiece. Allow three or four profiteroles per serving (see Favourite Recipes). Baking experience is required to produce a croquembouche, particularly in the making of the profiteroles, the caramel syrup and for the assembly.

Remember that as the profiteroles are cream-filled, appropriate storage conditions must be observed.

COMBINING CAKE BASES

Amongst other things, there is often the need to consider the likes and dislikes of principal guests - some may favour rich fruit, whilst others may prefer Madeira, calling for a compromise by making one or more tiers in rich fruit and one in Madeira. Another option would be to have a separate iced cake, known as a cutting cake, in an alternative cake base. Cutting cakes are iced but not decorated as they are not on display. They are used to provide extra portions or an alternative cake base and may also be useful if there are known allergies or special dietary requirements.

ICINGS, FILLINGS &
DECORATIVE PASTES

Although celebration cakes were traditionally royal iced, sugarpaste has become increasingly popular, largely due to the ease and speed with which it can be applied. Other variations, such as modelling chocolate and flavoured marzipan, are also becoming more widely used. This chapter sets out the different options to allow you to decide which cake covering you would prefer for taste and ease of application. It is also worth considering the different skills required for each.

Types of Icings and Coverings

Left: Three-tier stacked royal iced cake inspired by Renée Mackintosh

Royal Icing

Royal icing is made with sugar and egg white. Dried egg white powder - pure albumen - is often used in preference to raw egg white - fresh albumen - to minimize the potential risks associated with bacteria found in raw eggs. (However, certified salmonella-free eggs are available, see Chapter 11 - Making, Baking and Keeping.) Powdered albumen is simply reconstituted in water as per the instructions on the packet and is used in the same way as fresh egg white.

Royal icing can also be bought in ready-made powder form in packets to which water is simply added and mixed (see list of stockists).

Royal icing is regarded as a traditional method of cake decorating, but it can be used for classical and contemporary styles alike. It is only suitable for coating rich fruit cakes (and some semi-rich fruit cakes) as the marzipanned cake needs to be firm and stable for the icing to be applied. Once marzipanned, the cake should be left to dry for 24 hours (or up to, but no longer than, 48 hours) before the first coat of royal icing is applied. If the marzipan is left longer to dry out, the icing will break away from the marzipan when cut (a process called flinting).

A royal iced cake cannot be decorated quickly as the icing is applied in several thin coats - usually three - and is allowed to dry in-between. For this reason you should allow sufficient time for decoration. The finished surface should be smooth, even and level, and when cut into, the texture of the icing should be light and smooth. The icing can also be coloured if required using liquid or glycerine-free paste food colour.

The icing coating the top and sides of a cake is referred to as flat icing. For flat icing and ordinary piping work you can also use a fortified albumen, which is a blend of albumen and starches. It is prepared in the same way as royal icing made with fresh egg white or pure dried albumen and the result is a slightly whiter icing which, when dried, tends to be lighter in texture. It is less expensive than the pure form, but for any icing work where strength or stretch is required, for example, run out work, lace and extension work and filigree, only pure albumen is suitable as it is stronger and finished pieces are less fragile.

The final thickness of the icing should be approximately 3mm/^{1}/$_8$" in total.

FOR BEST RESULTS

If royal icing is made correctly, it should be light and easy to cut. Royal icing containing glycerine will maintain a softer cutting and eating texture, especially when the cake is decorated many weeks ahead of time. As glycerine retards setting, it must not be added to royal icing for run out or lace work.

The icing used for each coat must be properly beaten, of the same recipe, contain the same amount of glycerine (if used), and left to dry before the next coat is applied. This will ensure the layers of icing bond together properly and do not flake away from each other when the cake is cut (this is known as slating).

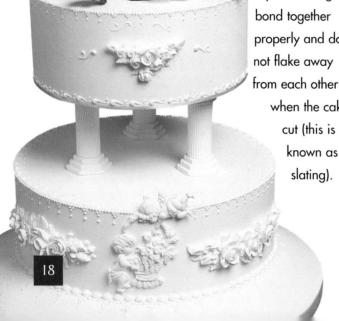

Dry each layer away from damp, humid or steamy conditions as this can cause blemishes on the finished icing.

Avoid using too much alcohol in the cake. Alcohol is best drizzled over the cake approximately ^{1}/$_2$ - 1^1/$_2$ hours after baking, when the cake is tepid. When thoroughly cold, the cake can then be wrapped and stored in a strong cardboard box ready for use. Too much alcohol added to the cake can cause it to become soggy and the excess moisture can then seep through the marzipan and discolour the finished royal icing.

There is something special about a royal iced cake - the pristine finish, the deliciously light, almost melt-in-the-mouth texture of the icing, the wonderful taste of a good marzipan beneath, and all finished with a rich moist fruit cake which is so very irresistible!

So, for this type of icing you need:-

• To allow yourself plenty of time for decorating and drying each layer

• Experience and skill for the work involved

• A rich fruit cake base pre-coated with marzipan

ROYAL ICING RECIPE

450g/1lb sieved icing sugar

75ml/3 fl oz albumen, sieved (egg white)

Please note that wherever fresh egg white is referred to, only guaranteed salmonella-free eggs should be used.

METHOD

1. Ensure that all tools and equipment are scrupulously clean as any traces of fat or grease will prevent aeration. If using fresh egg white, place into a bowl and, if possible, leave overnight. This will produce a stronger icing.

2. Beat the whites with two thirds of the sieved sugar - the mixture should be thick and white. Add the remaining sugar and continue to beat.

3. Beat the icing until the desired consistency is reached. This could take up to ten minutes when making royal icing by hand. The icing can also be made in a machine using the beater attachment: use the slowest speed possible, otherwise too many air bubbles will be incorporated, giving a rough surface when used to cover a cake and causing breaks when piping. Well-made royal icing should be light in consistency, not creamy and glossy which would indicate underbeating.

4. Keep the remaining icing covered with a clean damp cloth whilst working, and there-after in an airtight container. Alternatively, seal the bowl you are using with cling film, ensuring that no air can reach the icing. If royal icing is exposed to the air, a crust will form on the top. If the tiny pieces of crust are then beaten back into the icing, they will cause flat icing to have an uneven surface and cause piping tubes to block.

5. Store either in the refrigerator or in a very cool place. I would recommend using icing within three days.

6. To use the icing again, beat either by hand or machine (again using the slowest speed) for a couple of minutes. This allows air bubbles to be dispersed and for the mixture to be brought back to the correct consistency.

For very fine piping (i.e. anything with a no. 00 or 0 tube), sieve the icing through a piece of fine stocking mesh, ensuring you use the lightest possible shade and wash the mesh thoroughly before use. Squeeze the icing through the fabric. (Remember to put the mesh into the washing machine afterwards to ensure it is thoroughly clean. It can then be re-used again.)

USING ALBUMEN

Powdered pure albumen (egg white) rather than fresh egg white is now generally used for royal icing and unless the manufacturer's instructions say otherwise, is reconstituted in the following way:-

15g/$^1/_2$oz powdered albumen

100ml/3fl oz water

Add the albumen to the water and whisk in immediately. It will start off as a thick lumpy mass, but do not worry as this is normal. Leave the mixture to stand for approximately $1^1/_2$ - 2 hours, by which time the lumps should have dissolved. Strain before use to eliminate any remaining tiny albumen lumps. (This quantity will take approximately 500g/1lb 1oz icing sugar.)

Fortified powdered albumen is often used when making royal icing. It is less expensive than powdered (pure) albumen but contains starches and bulking agents which reduce the strength and stretch which is present in a pure albumen. It is excellent for flat icing and straightforward general piping work. It is not suitable for run-outs, lace or extension work, or wherever a strong royal icing is required.

GLYCERINE

Glycerine can be added to royal icing to maintain a softer cutting texture. Add one or two 5ml teaspoons to each 450g/1lb icing sugar used. As glycerine retards the setting of icing, thus keeping it softer, it must not be used for run-out, lace or filigree work.

ROYAL ICING CONSISTENCIES

For flat icing a cake, the consistency of royal icing should be *soft peak* - similar to a soft whipped double cream.

For piping, the icing needs to be a little stiffer to enable it to hold its own shape for piping shells, scrolls, writing and other fine piping work.

My personal preference is for royal icing made with a fortified albumen for flat icing (coating the cake) and simple piping as I find the texture is slightly lighter when cut into. For other work where strength is needed I would use a royal icing made with pure dried albumen. The exception to this is for extension work: I use only fresh egg white as I find it gives more stretch and flexibility.

MARZIPAN

Golden marzipan

Neutral marzipan

Nut-free 'marzipan'

Marzipan provides an excellent base for applying royal icing, sugarpaste and other similar cake coverings. It is available in a neutral ('white') and a golden colour ('yellow'). I have found that the flavour of the golden marzipan can be artificial and leave an aftertaste when eaten, so I prefer to use the neutral marzipan. Moreover, the neutral colour is much better for covering cakes and for modelling, and will take colour more easily. Raw sugar marzipan, which is almost brown in colour, is also available and can be purchased from some sugarcraft shops and health food stores.

Different brands do vary considerably in texture and taste so if you are not used to using marzipan, it is worthwhile tasting a number of different brands to find which you prefer. A good quality marzipan has a smooth texture which is easy to

roll out and a high almond content (a minimum of 23.5%) which gives it an excellent taste. 'Nut coverings' may contain a lower proportion of almonds or a combination of almonds and other nuts, but I always find that buying a high quality marzipan with excellent taste is well worthwhile. Many supermarkets may only stock one or two brands, so visit your local sugarcraft shop for alternatives. Marzipan has a long shelf life and stores easily. Once opened, wrap in strong polythene and keep airtight.

Home-made almond paste can also be used but there are a number of factors to consider. You will need to make a large quantity for a celebration cake, and it is not always as easy to roll out as a commercial paste. If the nuts used are oily or of poor quality, royal icing which is applied onto it can become stained as the oil and the colour seep through. Nowadays, some of the better quality commercial marzipans are just as good as home-made equivalents in consistency, taste, colour and handling. For those with nut allergies, an alternative nut-free 'marzipan' recipe is given in the Favourite Recipes section (page 138), together with a marzipan recipe should you wish to make your own.

CHOCOLATE MARZIPAN

This is made by kneading together equal amounts of marzipan and modelling chocolate (Cocoform). It provides an excellent base for rolled coverings and can also be used on its own. Chocolate marzipan is particularly useful when pouring melted chocolate over a cake as it

provides a smooth, level surface to work on (thus eliminating the problem of cake crumbs on the surface). Once the modelling chocolate and marzipan are blended, chocolate marzipan can be used (and stored) in the same way as ordinary marzipan.

Did You Know...?

Cornflour, also known as cornstarch, has many uses including thickening, as an ingredient in baking and even for making a stronger flour softer. More importantly for sugarcrafters, it is often used whilst making sugar flowers and for sugar modelling to prevent the paste from sticking to the board. However, when you are covering a cake, cornflour (or ordinary flour) should not be used to roll out either marzipan, sugarpaste or other similar roll-out coverings as it can cause a reaction between the marzipan and the cake which may result in the cake starting to form a mould. This mould ferments and a build up of gases starts to form. The cake may appear to have a small air bubble beneath the icing which will not disappear. This will grow as more gases form underneath and eventually, in extreme cases, the cake can explode! (I have only seen this happen once to a student who had rolled out marzipan on a worktop previously used for making bread dough.)

Do be certain that work surfaces, boards, rolling pins and any tools to be used are thoroughly cleaned and only use icing sugar for rolling out marzipan, sugarpaste and other roll-out coverings.

If you are rolling out dark coloured pastes, icing sugar can leave dusty patches even when the greatest care is taken. I find the easiest way to avoid this is to roll out the paste on a board lightly greased with white vegetable fat.

SUGARPASTE

Sugarpaste is extremely popular because of its relative ease of use: the paste is simply rolled out and the cake covered. It can be used on virtually any type of cake base.

Compared to royal icing, less time is needed to achieve a smooth, even, high standard of finish. It is easier to buy ready-made sugarpaste than to make your own as the texture, colour and flavour should be consistent, though the quality, taste and texture will differ slightly between brands.

Supermarkets usually only have 500g and 1kg packs and often only in white, but larger quantities and colour choice are available from your sugarcraft supplier. Sugarpaste has a long shelf life and is easily stored. Once opened, wrap well in a strong polythene bag, overwrap with cling film and keep airtight.

Although I would generally recommend buying ready-made sugarpaste, if you do wish to make your own, details can be found in Favourite Recipes (page 139).

So, for this type of icing the benefits are:-

• Cakes can be completed in advance

• Rich fruit or sponge type cake bases can be used

• Buttercream can be used to replace marzipan on Madeira and sponge cakes and marzipan can be

Cake covered with chocolate marzipan and chocolate sugarpaste. Hand modelled roses are made from Cocoform (modelling chocolate)

eliminated on rich fruit and semi-rich fruit cakes by using a double layer of sugarpaste (although this reduces keeping times)

- Less time is required to cover a cake with sugarpaste compared to royal icing

CHOCOLATE SUGARPASTE

This is an increasingly popular choice and can be used in the same way as plain sugarpaste to cover not only chocolate cakes but other flavoured cake bases such as vanilla, coffee and orange.

Chocolate sugarpaste made with cocoa is available, or you can make your own by blending equal amounts of Cocoform and sugarpaste.

BUTTERCREAM

Buttercream can also be used for covering cakes, though it is more commonly used for filling and coating sponge cakes prior to sugarpasting. It can be made in a number of ways, but the most popular recipe is a mix of butter and icing sugar beaten together to form a light fluffy consistency

(see Favourite Recipes, page 136). Some of the unsalted continental butters give a much more distinctive, creamier taste and it is worthwhile trying a few to find which you prefer. Hot sunny days and long car journeys are not buttercream friendly, so the cake needs to be kept cool.

So, when covering a cake using buttercream:-

- Inevitably, there will be a considerable amount of last minute work.

- It is not suitable for rich fruit or semi-rich fruit cakes

- It is very popular with children

- It can also be used as the filling for a dessert cake

GANACHE

Ganache is a mixture of chocolate and cream which is used as a filling, as a covering and for piping on cakes. The consistency of ganache can be altered by varying the ratio of cream to chocolate: more chocolate will give a thicker mix

and a firmer set. Using the very best quality chocolate is reflected in the taste and is certainly worthwhile. The taste can be further enhanced with flavourings, for example, coffee or orange liqueur. As it contains cream, ganache needs to be prepared

at the last minute and kept at a cool temperature. (See Favourite Recipes, page 137 for making instructions.)

So, when using ganache:-

• A considerable amount of last minute work is involved

• The rich chocolate covering (and filling) is very popular

• It can also be used as a filling for a dessert cake

• It needs to be kept cool even whilst transporting

CHOCOLATE COUVERTURE

A high-quality smooth eating chocolate with a fine flavour. When used for coating, pouring or other decorations, couverture will not produce a high quality gloss unless it is tempered. Tempering is a process which involves heating the complex mixture of fats in chocolate, which have different melting and setting points, to specific temperatures at which they become compatible with each other. It will then produce the high gloss and 'snap' associated with good quality chocolate. (Before attempting to temper chocolate, make sure you have correct instructions as it is a process which demands accuracy. You will find details on couverture packs or in specialist books such as Hanneman's Patisserie Book.) Couverture can be purchased in blocks, pieces or as drops from sugarcraft shops, wholesalers, or by mail order.

Please do remember that chocolate melts at a low temperature, so hot sunny days will hasten the melting process.

CHOCOLATE CURLS (CARAQUE)

An excellent and convenient way to provide a high standard of decoration to a chocolate cake, these can be bought ready-made to save you hours of making your own. They are available in dark, milk or white chocolate. As the curls are fragile, they are not available through mail order. Make sure you order well in advance and follow the manufacturer's instructions for storage.

If you do wish to make your own chocolate curls, melt some good quality chocolate (if you are using

it to scrape across the chocolate to produce the curls (caraque). (The method is similar to that of making butter curls.) I would not recommend using synthetically flavoured baking chocolate for making chocolate curls because, due to its soft texture, it does not curl easily.

So, for chocolate covered cakes:

- Last minute work is inevitable

- You can create a superb table centrepiece

- They can be served as a dessert

- Chocolate needs to be kept cool even whilst transporting

couverture, temper first for best results) and pour onto a board. Once the chocolate starts to harden, hold the blade of a sharp flat-edged knife or palette knife horizontally with both hands and use

MODELLING CHOCOLATE

Modelling chocolate (also known as 'plastic chocolate') is available ready-made under the name Cocoform in dark, milk and white and in colours of green, red, blue and yellow. It is ideal for making flowers, figures, moulded decorations, and novelty work and can be blended with an equal amount of marzipan to make 'chocolate marzipan' (as described above). A basic modelling paste is simply a combination of liquid glucose and couverture (see Favourite Recipes on page 140).

FILLINGS FOR CAKES

The choice of filling for any cake is down to personal preference. The most popular choices are buttercream, jam (jelly) and ganache (or similar chocolate filling). Buttercreams can be used on their own or with jam, and can be flavoured the same as the sponge base or with a complementary flavour, for example, coffee and almond or chocolate and peppermint. Ganache, when made with best chocolate and rich double cream, often needs no further additions, but the use of a few drops of coffee or orange liqueur can provide additional flavour, especially when used with a plain sponge cake. The advantage of both buttercream and ganache is that they are relatively firm fillings. If sugarpaste or another roll-out covering is to be used, the weight of the paste can cause soft fillings to bulge out at the sides of the cake resulting in an uneven and poor standard of finish. There are many recipes for delicious cake fillings and it is worthwhile having a look through cookery books and magazines for different and appealing ideas and then trying them out. The point to consider would be their suitability in the type of celebration cake required and the covering being used.

JAM

Jam (also known as 'jelly') can be purchased in a wide range of flavours. The higher quality jams have good flavour and a reasonable amount of fruit content, although I do not think anything can compare with home-made jam. When used in sponges, jams can provide additional flavour, either when used on their own or as a combination with buttercream. Do be certain the amount of filling overall will not bulge at the sides when the weight from the covering is applied.

Apricot jam is also used as a glaze between the marzipan and the cake, simply because it has the most neutral flavour and colour. 225g/8oz of apricot jam is boiled, with two tablespoons of water or lemon juice, and sieved before being brushed onto the cake (this can be done in a microwave oven or in a saucepan on the stove). The glaze should be brushed onto the cake when it is piping hot as this helps reduce the possibility of mould growth.

The marzipan/almond paste should be rolled ready to place over the jam as soon as it has been applied to the cake as this helps to form a good seal. Only apply the smallest amount of jam to cover the surface of the cake as too much will result in a soggy mess and the moisture can start to dissolve the marzipan.

If you decide to use a ready-made apricot glaze, I would advise you to boil it in the same way as traditional jam.

DECORATIVE PASTES

FLOWER PASTE

Flower paste is most commonly used to create sugar flowers and leaves as the paste can be rolled finely to produce realistic floral work. It is also known as Sugar Florist Paste and Petal Paste and is available in a wide range of ready-made colours as well as black and white. Different manufacturers will have their own colour ranges. You can use the paste straight from the packet or mix it with other colours. Different brands tend to have different handling qualities, so find one that suits you. The ready-made colours are particularly useful when making dark coloured flowers or leaves or with modelling work, as it is often far easier to start with a similar base colour to the one you want and then mix in other colours to achieve a match (refer to the colour wheel in Chapter 8). Adding a large amount of paste colour to white flower paste can alter the consistency, so if you need to obtain a dark colour, try using extra strength colours as a lesser amount of colour needs to be added to the paste. Alternatively, if suitable, paint or dust over your finished work when dried to achieve the depth of colour required.

If you wish to make your own flower paste, there are many recipes to be found in sugarcraft books and there will be a great variation in ingredients. Many people have their own favourite recipe but if you have not made your own before, try out a few recipes to find one that suits you (a suggestion can be found in Favourite Recipes, page 139).

MODELLING PASTE

Again, many recipes exist and often people make their own simply by mixing sugarpaste and flower paste together. The proportions will depend upon the use: equal amounts of each will give a fairly firm consistency; for a softer paste, use 75% sugarpaste and 25% flower paste. Adding gum tragacanth to sugarpaste also produces a modelling paste (see Favourite Recipes, page 140). (For details on modelling chocolate, see page 27.)

PASTILLAGE

Used extensively for modelling work especially plaques, buildings, backdrops, arches, cradles, and caskets, pastillage is very strong and hard when dried. Pastillage is usually rolled out and cut to the shape required using templates and left to dry. For built-up modelling work, e.g. buildings, caskets and scenes, the pieces are joined together with royal icing.

CHOOSING SHAPES
FOR YOUR CAKES

The shape of a cake will very much depend on personal preference. When you are planning your design, consider the full range of shapes available to you - everything from round and square to ovals, diamonds, triangles, teardrops, hexagons, octagons and their elongated versions, plus many more in-between.

TINS

Shaped cake tins are available in various sizes, allowing you to put together a well balanced multi-tiered cake or provide you with an appropriate-sized single tier. The widest range of cake tin sizes offered will be for round and square shapes - from 10cm/4" to 40.5cm/16" - but if you have a slimline oven, make sure any larger sized tin will fit in.

It is usually more economical to hire cake tins than to buy them - especially unusual shaped ones - from a sugarcraft shop. However, it may be worth buying them if you are going to use them frequently. If you decide to hire your tins, do arrange to hire them well in advance. Before you take them back, make a template of the tin using thin card: this can then be used to help with design and, more importantly, will be needed for the positioning of any pillars/dowels being used.

An important point to bear in mind when choosing tins is that hexagonal and octagonal tins are measured point-to-point, whilst the boards are measured side to side. It helps if you are aware of this when hiring tins and ordering boards.

COMBINING SHAPES

Combining different shaped cakes within the same design can be very effective. It is worth considering combinations such as square and round, hexagon and heart, and oval and teardrop or scalloped oval.

When combining shapes in a multi-tiered cake, consider the widest diameter measurement of each tier to ensure the finished design will be well balanced. If necessary, adjust the cake sizes so that the higher the tier, the smaller the cake. For example, a 20cm/8" square would not appear well balanced above a 25.5cm/10" round base as the 20cm/8" square measures over 28cm/11" at the widest point. This could easily be rectified by using either an 18cm/7" square at the top or swapping the shapes around so the base is a 25.5cm (10") square and the upper tier a 20cm/8" round (this would also enable the upper tier size to be increased to a 23cm/9" round).

CREATING YOUR OWN SHAPES

For something unique, why not cut the cake to your own design? Boards can be cut to match the cake, or a complementary board shape can be used.

These are just a few examples of basic shapes which can be used to create unusual designs.

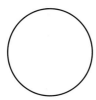 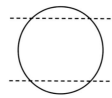

A plain round cake trimmed to create two flat areas. The flat areas create focal points and are particularly useful for emphasizing decoration.

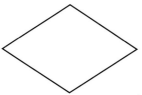 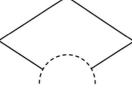 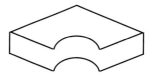

Diamond shaped cake with a semi-circle cut out. This would provide a specific area for decoration.

 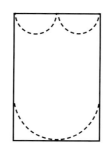 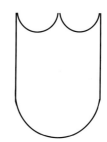

Plain rectangular cake cut to the shape of a shield. This could provide the ideal background for a family crest or coat of arms. This shape cake would be particularly suitable for a themed wedding held in a castle.

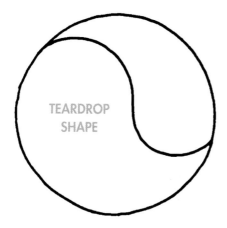

TEARDROP SHAPE

HOW MANY
PORTIONS & HOW
MANY CAKES?

Having decided upon the type of cake base and shape of your cakes, the next point to consider is how many portions you will need to serve, which will, of course, determine the overall quantity and sizes of the cakes to be made.

PORTIONS

HOW MANY GUESTS?

Working out how many portions of cake you need is generally based on the number of guests at the celebration. There may also be guests who are not able to attend and others who have not been invited but with whom the cake will be shared such as work colleagues, neighbours and acquaintances.

Often, particularly with weddings, the celebrations run on into the evening with a further set of guests arriving. Try to ascertain just when the cake will be cut and shared amongst the guests: if it is at the main wedding meal and again in the evening when both sets of guests are present, nearly double the amount of portions will be required.

These days, many bridal couples choose to make the traditional first cut into the cake, then allow the cake to remain on show until the evening when it is cut up and shared amongst all the guests. This is fine unless it is a chocolate cake filled with ganache with a cream based covering on a hot sunny day! Reassess the cake base choice at this stage, or have one cake out and a separate cutting cake in the fridge.

So, remember to include all the following sets of people when calculating the number of portions required:-

- Guests attending the celebration

- Guests attending an evening function

- Guests unable to attend

- Others not invited to whom cake will be given or posted

CAKE BASES

When you know how many portions are required, the size of the cake required will depend on the type of cake base being used.

A rich fruit cake will yield the most portions as it is firm and will cut into small pieces without crumbling. It is normally divided into 2.5cm/1" squares on the top, then cut straight down to give oblong pieces. (Please note that the Portion Guide Chart on page 128 allows for 2.5cm/1" square pieces.)

As it has a less dense texture, a Madeira or other similar type of cake needs to be cut into larger portions otherwise it will break up. It is normally cut into portions of 4cm/1^1/$_2$" square or 5cm x 2.5cm/2" x 1" rectangles.

Where the cake is to be used as a dessert, for example, a chocolate or strawberry sponge, the cake bases can be made slightly deeper to accommodate larger portions. You will then probably find that a 5cm x 2.5cm/2" x 1" slice is sufficient. Alternatively, use the figure for the sponge portions, decrease it by 15% to 20% and cut into slightly larger portions,

e.g. 50 sponge portions - 15% = 42 dessert portions

The Portion Guide Chart on page 128 will help you to determine the amounts that can be obtained from regular and irregular shaped cakes in either rich fruit or sponge.

HOW TO CUT A CAKE

The way in which a cake is cut will also have a bearing on the amount of portions obtained. I find it easiest to use a sharp serrated knife. First, mark points along the edges of the cake with the end of the knife at the required intervals (as desribed

above), then make cuts across the cake followed by cuts down the cake. It is important to wipe the blade clean after each cut to ensure a clean, sharp cut each time. A guide on cutting your cake is given below.

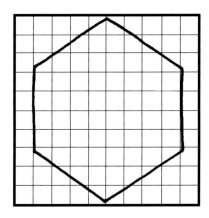
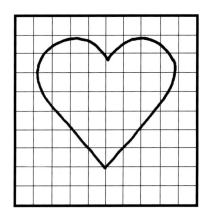
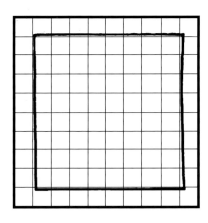
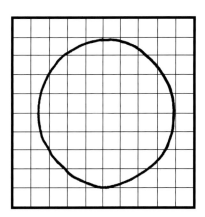

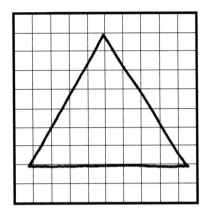

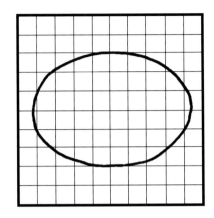

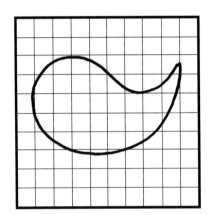

There will inevitably be some wastage when the cake is cut, so do allow for this when planning your design.

EXTRA PORTIONS - CUTTING CAKES

If there is a high number of guests, the cake you are planning to make may not provide sufficient portions for everyone. An ideal solution is to use an additional cutting cake.

A cutting cake is iced but not decorated (it is not on display) and is cut up at the same time as the wedding/celebration cake, providing the extra portions required. The cutting cake can be the same or a different cake base to

the wedding/celebration cake. In addition, it can also be used where an alternative type of cake is to be offered to the guests.

QUANTITIES

CAKE MIX

Cake recipes do not usually give the varying quantities required for different shapes and sizes of cakes, so a foolproof way of calculating the mix required for any size cake is essential. A sure way of determining how much cake mix will be needed for a certain size cake is to check what size cake the recipe you are using will produce. If, for example, the recipe states that the cake is sufficient for a 20cm/8" round, then fill a 20cm/8" round cake tin with water to the level the cake mix would normally reach. Tip this into the tin size you intend to use and continue until the tin you are using is filled to the same point. Keep a record of how many tins of water are needed to fill the cake tin: this is the figure you will need to multiply the basic recipe by to obtain sufficient cake mix.

If, however, you need the information before you hire the cake tins, the chart on page 132 provides guidelines on the amounts of cake mix needed for different shapes and sizes of tins. Do remember, however, that recipes differ. If you are unsure, make more mix, and any left over can be made into a small gift cake.

QUANTITIES OF MARZIPAN, ROYAL ICING AND SUGARPASTE (OR SIMILAR COVERINGS)

The method for working out the quantities of marzipan and royal icing needed to cover a rich fruit cake is often determined by weight. The rich fruit cake is weighed and the amount of marzipan required will be 50% of the total weight. The same rule applies for royal icing or sugarpaste. For example, a 1.81kg/4lb cake would require 900g/2lb of marzipan and 900g/2lb of royal icing or sugarpaste. This will give a good marzipan coverage and sufficient royal icing for three coats, plus a little for decoration.

A cake which is to be royal iced should have a minimum of 0.7cm/$^1/_4$" layer of marzipan on the top and a minimum of 0.3cm/$^1/_8$" on the sides. The thickness can certainly be increased to suit personal tastes. (In days gone by, it was the norm for marzipan to be 2cm/$^3/_4$" to 2.5cm/1" thick on the top of the cake!)

Working out the amount of marzipan for other cake bases is not quite so straghtforward! The Quantity Charts on page 129 give guidelines on the amounts of marzipan, royal icing and sugarpaste needed to cover cakes of various shapes and sizes.

PILLARS, STANDS
& SEPARATORS

An elegant tall pillar can be used to add height to a cake

The way in which you assemble a cake is a crucial part of the design process. Whether you choose to use pillars, separators, dividers, a cake stand, or a completely original alternative such as candlesticks, goblets or even a silver trophy belonging to the bride or groom, always ensure the assembly of the cake complements its design. The contemporary cake decorator has an enormous choice in the overall design and presentation of a cake - the possiblities are virtually endless. We will look at some of these choices individually, starting with the use and presentation of pillars.

PILLARS

Pillars now come in a wide range of shape, size, colour and materials and can enhance a cake superbly. Whatever style of pillar is chosen, their function is to separate and support the tiers of a wedding or celebration cake.

It should be noted that cakes often need the support not only of pillars, but also of dowels to properly support the cake. The process of dowelling cakes is fully explained in the following chapter.

PLASTER PILLARS

These can be coloured as required using food colours, dusting powders, and lustre colours, and they can be 'gilded' using edible metallic colours. If the design of the cake means that the pillar(s) will come into contact with any part of the cake, the colours you use must be edible. Pillars can be coloured with dusting powder using a large soft brush, but be careful to remove any excess dust as this could fall onto the icing and spoil the finish of the cake. It is for this reason I find it useful not to dust the base of the pillar.

To 'gild' a pillar, first brush with a light coating of Gildesol. Using a clean soft brush, dust over the pillar with your chosen edible metallic colour, then burnish with a clean, dry brush to highlight the colour and to remove excess powder. The same method applies to other lustre colours, which when used with Gildesol, will result in a more intense colour than when simply dusted directly onto the pillar. It is a good idea to colour the pillars after dowelling the cakes: handling dusted pillars whilst dowelling cakes can result in accidentally marking the icing as excess dust can easily be transferred to your fingers.

Plaster pillars come in a wide range of shapes and sizes, but some of the specialized pillars need to be ordered well in advance. Plaster pillars are solid, but some of the newer designer ranges come with a dowel hole in the bottom which makes dowelling a cake much easier.

PLASTIC PILLARS

These usually come in white, cream, gold and silver, as well as in different shapes and sizes. They are difficult to colour because edible food colours will not adhere to plastic. Try decorating them with tiny co-ordinating sugar flowers or leaves, or use coloured ribbon or other trimmings instead. The plastic pillars will take ordinary non-edible paints, but as these are non-edible and most of them toxic, it is certainly not recommended for use with cakes.

PASTILLAGE PILLARS

You can make your own pillars using pastillage to create a unique design and, like the plaster ones, they are easily coloured and decorated. However, cake size should be taken into consideration here as pastillage pillars may not be suitable for larger or heavier cakes owing to their relative fragility.

PERSPEX PILLARS

These are often more contemporary in design than traditional pillars. Designs presented as clear hollow 'tubes' have an added advantage as the tubes can be filled with tiny coloured glass balls or beads, gossamer fine patterned craft paper/fabric, or the celebration party table decorations. Perspex pillars will normally need to be specially ordered.

SILVER PLATED PILLARS

Silver pillars are extremely elegant, beautifully crafted and the most expensive because of the material they are made from and the high standard of finish. They can only be purchased to special order and you will need to ascertain which sizes and shapes are available before planning your design.

How To Use Pillars

The positioning of pillars on a cake is not guesswork: they are spaced at specific intervals from the centre of the cake so that when used in conjunction with dowels, they provide an even distribution of weight and maximum support and stability.

Some cakes, for example round or oval, look equally good with either three or four pillars, so the number of pillars used in these cases will largely depend on personal choice. Other shapes tend to be more suited to a specific number of pillars, for example, a square cake would normally have four to a tier. Remember to make allowances for the position of pillars when preparing any design work for the top of the lower tiers of your cake and ensure the height of the pillars is sufficient to accommodate any sugar flowers or decorative pieces.

With multi-tiered cakes, taller pillars can be used on the lower tiers, with slightly shorter ones for the upper tiers, to give an evenly balanced appearance overall.

Positioning Of Pillars (and Dowels)

The position of the pillars is calculated according to the diameter of the cake. This ensures maximum stability and a well-balanced appearance. We will deal with both regular and irregular shaped cakes.

The pillar chart on page 130 gives the positions for both three and four pillars on a cake for a variety of sizes. Once you know the central point on the cake, the positioning chart is straightforward to use. If you have a larger cake than is specified on the chart, simply extend the circles and lines using the given chart as a guide. It is a good idea to photocopy the chart and laminate it or cover it in sticky backed plastic, so it is then ready to use whenever you need it. This way, it can also be wiped clean after use.

SQUARE, OCTAGONAL AND ROUND: FOUR PILLARS

.... Fold lines to locate centre of cake and position pillars

.... Fold lines to locate centre of cake using alternative position pillars

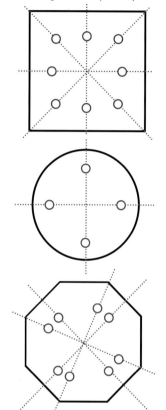

(Remember that for square and octagonal cakes, pillars can be positioned in line with the corners or in line with the sides of the cake.)

METHOD 1

1. Make a template of each of your cakes (except the top tier) from thin card or paper.

2. Fold each template in half and in half again to locate the centre, then open out. For square and octagonal cakes, you can fold the template in half corner-to-corner or side-to-side, depending on your design.

3. Measure the diameter of each cake. Using the pillar chart, mark the correct distance for the pillars from the centre of your template onto each fold line.

4. Return your template to the top of the cake and mark where the pillars are to be placed using a scriber.

METHOD 2

Alternatively, mark the centre of your cake using the templates, then place the pillar chart in the centre of your cake and mark where the pillars are to be placed according to the diameter.

HEXAGONAL, ROUND AND PETAL: THREE PILLARS

.... Fold lines to locate centre of cake

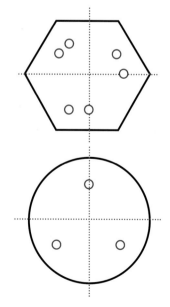

For these shapes, the pillars are positioned at three evenly spaced intervals. As a complete circle is 360°, each section will be 120°.

METHOD 1

1. Make a template (as described above) and fold twice to locate the centre. (You will not use these fold lines for positioning the pillars this time.)

2. Transfer the template to the pillar chart and mark on the three points for the pillars according to the diameter of the cake. The chart gives you three 120° sections, indicated by the dotted line.

3. Transfer the template to the cake and mark the three pillar positions with a scriber.

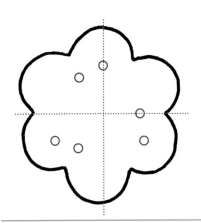

METHOD 2

Alternatively, take the pillar chart, locate the centre with the template, place the chart in the centre of the cake and mark where the pillars should go (according to the size of the cake) using the dotted lines.

For petal and hexagonal shapes, use the widest points as the diameter measurement as greater stability is obtained in this way, although pillars for both petal and hexagonal can be placed in either of the positions indicated.

OVAL, DIAMOND AND ELONGATED OCTAGONAL: FOUR PILLARS

.... Fold lines to locate centre of cake and position pillars

.... Fold lines to locate centre of cake using alternative position pillars

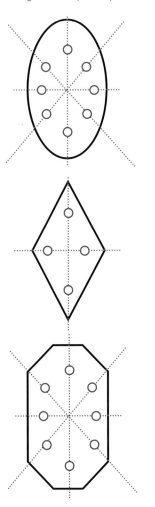

To position pillars on these shapes, the measurements both lengthways and widthways are used. This method allows pillars on irregular shaped cakes to be placed at the correct distance from the centre of the cake.

Alternative positions for the pillars, on the diagonal, are also indicated. However, on the diamond shape I would only recommend positioning the pillars facing the points of the cake for stability. Furthermore, on smaller cakes, the overall appearance can look too fussy.

METHOD 1

1. Make templates as before.

2. Decide in which position the pillars will be placed, then fold the template in half and in half again. Open out.

3a. For the blue positions, measure the length widthways and, using this measurement, refer to the pillar chart to mark the template with the correct pillar positions. Repeat for the lengthways positions. Place the template centrally onto the cake and transfer the marks.

3b. For the red positions fold the template as before. Fold again as shown. Open up, measure the length diagonally and, using this measurement, refer to the pillar chart and mark the pillar positions. Transfer the positions to the cake.

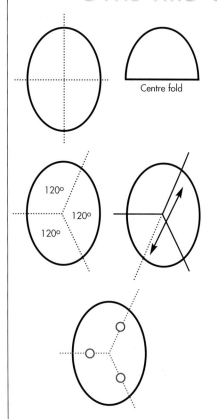

OVAL AND ELLIPTICAL: THREE PILLARS

Centre fold

120°
120°
120°

Yet more choices! The oval is a very versatile shape and can be tiered with either three or four pillars. The choice is a personal one, but think about any decoration and whether three or four pillars will best complement the design.

METHOD

1. Make a template of your cake and fold to locate the centre.

2. Fold the template in half widthways and measure the length along the straight line. Using this measurement, refer to the pillar chart and mark one pillar position on the template.

3. Working from the centre of your template, divide it into three 120° sections by placing on the pillar chart and using the dotted lines as a guide (or use a protractor using the centre fold as the start of the first section).

4. Measure the diagonal length and using this measurement mark the final two pillar positions onto your template. Transfer all three to your cake.

TRIANGLE

For greatest stability, place the pillars on triangular cakes opposite the points.

METHOD

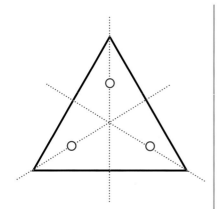

1. Make a template of your cake as before and fold to locate the centre.

2. Measure the distance along one of the folds, from the centre of one side to the point. This is the 'diameter' measurement.

3. Using the chart, mark the pillar positions and transfer these to your cake.

HEART

The heart shape needs a little more work when calculating the best pillar positions but I have found the following method to be a reliable and relatively easy way of doing so.

METHOD

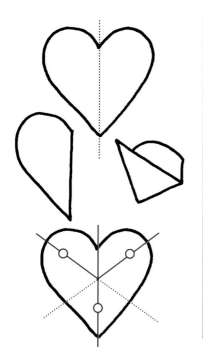

1. Make a template of the cake and fold in half.

2. Take the point across template until it is level with the top curve, keeping the side edges more or less lined up, and fold. This will give you the centre point of the cake.

3. Draw a line from the centre as shown and fold along this line. Open out the template and continue this line right across. This will give you the 'diameter' of your cake.

4. Using this measurement, refer to the pillar chart and mark three pillar positions. Transfer to your cake.

TEARDROP

Teardrop shaped cakes are naturally beautiful with their elegant curved lines. However, due to the load bearing weight being at one side, I would not recommend the use of pillars. I also find that pillars tend to detract from the elegant shape of the teardrop, so it is far better to enhance teardrop cakes with the use of one of the substantial heavyweight decorative plaster pillars, a candle-stick, or perspex dividers/ separators. Alternatively, try displaying the cake at different angles or heights with soft material folds or drapes.

OTHER SHAPES

When creating your own shaped cakes, or using shapes not mentioned in this chapter, by using the methods previously described in relation to size and diameter you will be able to ascertain the best pillar positions for your cake to give stability and balance. Pillars may not be suitable with cakes cut to very irregular and non-symmetrical shapes: in these instances, consider cake stands as an alternative.

COMBINING SHAPES

Sometimes a design will include different shaped cakes for one or each of the tiers. Consider the pillar positions for each of the shapes to best suit the design. Some will go very easily together such as round and heart, round and hexagonal, or square and octagonal. With others, you may be able to use three pillars instead of four or vice versa, for example when using a square with a round, or an elongated octagonal with an oval. Whatever your choice of pillars, it is important to ensure the finished cake is properly supported and the overall design well balanced.

CAKE STANDS

Cake stands can also be used to display a cake. There is an excellent choice of shape, size and colour and most cake stands are available to hire from sugarcraft shops. Charges for hiring cake stands will inevitably vary depending on the type of stand being hired. The greater the value of the stand, the greater the hire charge will usually be. A deposit is required for items hired which is refunded upon return, unless the item is lost or damaged in which case full replacement costs may be incurred. Items returned late may also incur further charges. Arrange to hire the cake stand you require well in advance, especially if it is needed over the weekend, and check the time limit. Most sugarcraft shops allow stands to be hired for three, four or five days. You can also buy stands but again, order early.

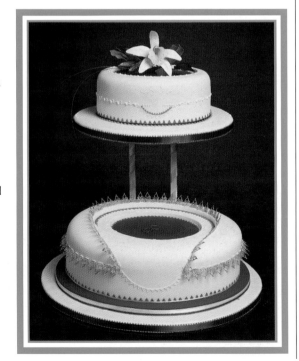

BASE CAKE STANDS

Base cake stands add the finishing touch to the presentation of a cake and can be used in conjunction with pillars, dividers or separators for a multi-tiered cake or on their own for stacked or single-tiered designs. They are available in both silver and gold colours in either a round or square shape. Silver plated stands are also available in both round and square, with oval ones being available to special order. They are very elegantly designed and finished to an extremely high standard. Again, order in advance and check the terms for hire.

MULTI-TIERED CAKE STANDS

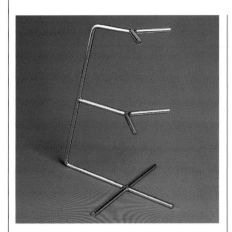

There is no doubt that multi-tiered cake stands are the easiest way to display a cake - no dowelling of the tiers is required, instead the tiers are simply placed onto the different levels the stand provides. These stands are available in chrome, gold colour chrome and perspex in an amazing array of shapes and sizes.

Chrome stands can be entwined with matching or co-ordinating ribbon. Tartan ribbon looks particularly good for a Scottish

wedding and can be even more personalised if you obtain the clan tartan ribbon of the bride and/or groom. You could have a completely plain cake with sugar, silk or fresh flowers attached to the stand. If you are very new to cake decorating you may wish to decorate the cake and ask the florist to decorate the stand.

Perspex stands also come in different styles and are particularly useful for their versatility in presentation.

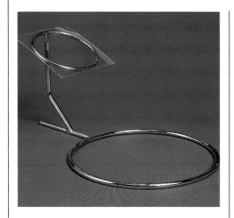

Tilting stands allow you to present one or more tiers tilted at an angle which can be very effective. They are used in conjunction with non-slip mats, which are placed onto the tilt and the cake is then placed onto the mat. The design on the top of the cake can be cleverly and clearly displayed in this way. Although stands will vary, I would not recommend using a tilted stand for a cake any bigger than 30.5cm/12".

Have a look in your local florist as some stands for flower arranging are excellent for cake decorating. The stand should not come into contact with the cake if it is not of food grade, but this can often be overcome by using food grade plastic separator discs between the stand and cake. Plastic separator discs are available from sugarcraft shops.

HOME-MADE STANDS

If you cannot find a cake stand to your liking, why not make your own? Base cake stands can be made easily using cake drums or MDF available from DIY stores. They can be built up to the height required with either even or graduated sides and their shape can match or co-ordinate with your cake. You can cover your home-made board in material, or use various painting techniques to create different effects such as ragging, gilding, sponging, or découpage. You can even put small feet on the MDF stands using decorative cupboard knobs. Remember to allow yourself enough time for this.

A custom-made two-tier cake stand

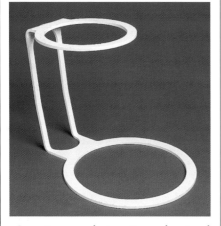

If you are lucky enough to live in an area where there is a blacksmiths or where metalcraft or woodturning is still practised, you may wish to think about having a stand made, but you will need to determine the cost beforehand. In the past, my brother-in-law has made me three cake stands, all enamelled in off-white, which I have used endlessly as the neutral colour blends in with most colour schemes and he was able to make them just as I wanted. If you are going to use them frequently, you may wish to have your own stands made, especially if you intend to progress to running a small business from home (see Chapter 13 - Selling Cakes from Home).

Separators And Dividers

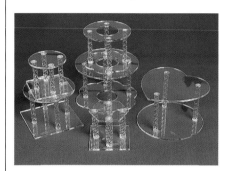

Separators are used in much the same way as pillars but are generally a larger, one-piece construction, often in perspex and sometimes in silver. (Contact your local sugarcraft shop for a catalogue.) Depending on the weight of the cakes, you may still need to dowel them for stability (and peace of mind). Do remember to make allowances for separators when designing any cake top decoration.

Separators are positioned centrally or where the load bearing is greatest. In the same way as when pillars are used, they should provide maximum support and stability.

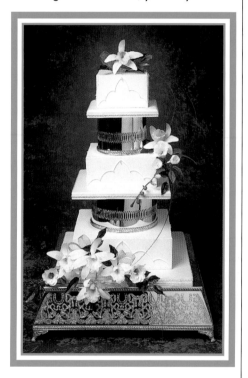

Large Designer Pillars

For smaller, single-tiered cakes, consider using a large (30.5cm/12") designer pillar as a cake stand, perhaps dusted in a lustre or satin finish to match bridal fabrics, or silver, pearl or golden wedding celebrations.

CANDLESTICKS

Candlesticks come in a variety of styles, shapes, sizes and heights, and their use in cake decoration can be very wide ranging indeed, offering different and unusual alternatives to pillars and cake stands. In this chapter we will be looking at their use in relation to pillars and stands. Farther on, we will look at their use in presentation.

Candlesticks provide a more unusual design aspect for a two tier cake. A single candlestick with a wide base and top can be used as a separator between tiers, depending on the size of the cake. They often come with a small spike on the top designed to secure a candle, which is ideal to secure your cake board! Remember that the candlestick must be of a suitable size to offer sufficient support in relation to the size of the cake.

For cakes with more than two tiers, three or four smaller candle holders in glass, silver or pewter, for example, can be used as pillars (again, with dowels). This provides more stability for larger cakes than a single candlestick. After the event, they could be offered as a gift and a memento of a special occasion.

A simple cake can be complemented well with a candlestick used to display flowers. Florists sell candle cups which are slotted into the top of a normal candlestick fitting and secured using flower arrangers' tape (very strong ribbed sticky tape). The candle cup is then filled with a malleable fixative material ready for you to arrange your flowers.

OTHER OPTIONS

There are many ornamental items that can also serve as cake separators, from small vases to simple figurines. Sometimes glasses or goblets can be used as separators, but care should be taken to ensure there is no risk that they may break and shatter glass over the cake. Whatever objects you choose, do ensure they are suitable, i.e. will not break, spoil or become damaged in any way, and will properly support the cake. The use of family heirlooms is not recommended!

If you do decide to use an object that is not specifically designed for cake decoration, it is important to use a plastic separator disc between the cake and the object.

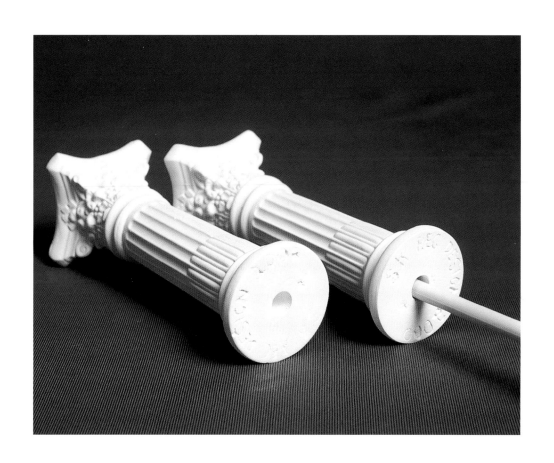

DOWELLING

CAKES

Having discussed the use of pillars and other separators, it is important to look at different types of dowels and how they are used. Pillars can make a cake look stunning, but it is no good if they sink into the cake!

WHY USE DOWELS?

Nearly all cakes, whether they are stacked or use pillars, are dowelled. When there is a large number of tiers, the weight taken by the base tier is very great. Sugarpaste, chocolate icing and similar coverings are quite soft, and pillars, separators or dividers, whilst helping to spread the weight taken by the lower tiers, may sink into the icing and subsequently cause the cake to topple. Sponge cakes of any type will not bear any great weight above them without support, so it is essential to dowel them correctly.

Rich fruit cakes are the most sturdy of all cake bases and when royal iced, may not require dowelling. Often, however, cakes are left on display for many hours, sometimes into the early evening before being taken down for cutting, so I always prefer to dowel a royal iced cake of two tiers or more. If glycerine has been added to the icing to maintain a softer cutting texture, dowels should always be used.

Another factor to consider is what the cake table will be standing on: garden marquees are becoming increasingly popular for celebrations, but just as a house without a damp proof course can become damp, so can a marquee. The moisture from the lawn beneath can cause a great deal of humidity, especially if the weather outside is wet. This in turn can affect the icing which may become softer than usual. If the cake is not dowelled there is a chance it may become unstable and possibly fall, particularly if the floor is not as stable as a permanent one! If in doubt, it is a good idea to dowel the cakes, just to give them some extra stability.

TYPES OF DOWEL

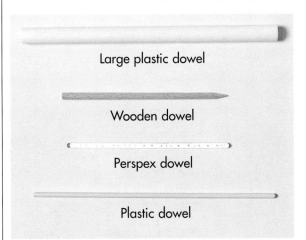

Large plastic dowel

Wooden dowel

Perspex dowel

Plastic dowel

Dowels can be used with pillars, separators and dividers and are available in plastic, perspex and wood. There are some pillars and separators which come with dowels (or spikes) attached, so have a look at what is available and choose whatever you prefer to use.

Left: Three-tier pillared cake with brush embroidery design

PLASTIC DOWELS

Plastic dowels are gently rounded at both ends for easy insertion into a cake. Once pushed into the cake, the rounded end will rest firmly against the cake board. These dowels may be cut with very little effort using heavy duty kitchen scissors, a strong serrated knife or a mini saw (hacksaw), which must be kept and used only for sugarcraft.

Some brands of kitchen scissors have shaped blades designed for cutting chicken bones. This type of scissor is ideal for cutting dowels and wires. Keep a pair solely for sugarcraft use to avoid cross contamination.

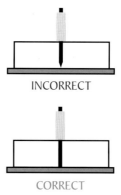

WOODEN DOWELS

Wooden dowels have one flat end and one sharp pointed end. The purpose of the pointed end is to allow the dowel to be inserted through the cake to the cake board without causing damage to the iced surface. It should not be left in this position, however, as when weight is applied to the dowel, the point could pierce and sink into the cake board. Therefore, once the dowel has been guided through the cake to the cake board with the pointed end, it should carefully be removed and inserted again with the flat end at the bottom.

Wooden dowels can be cut in the same way as plastic dowels, but be certain the cut is neat and clean to avoid splinters finding their way into the cake. To avoid this potential problem, I prefer to use plastic dowels.

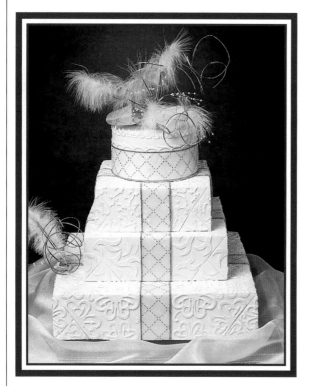

INCORRECT

CORRECT

HOW TO DOWEL A CAKE

HOLLOW PILLARS

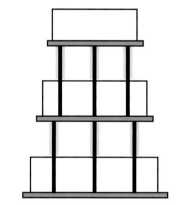

1. Mark the pillar/dowel positions on the cake (see previous chapter).

2. Insert the dowel vertically through the cake to the cake board using a gentle turning action. If you are using wooden dowels, remove and re-insert as described above.

3. Place a hollow pillar over the dowel and mark the dowel 1 or 2mm above the top of the pillar. This allows the weight of the upper tiers to rest on the dowels and not the pillars. Repeat with all pillars and dowels.

4. Remove the pillars and dowels. Cut the dowels to the required length and re-insert into the cake.

5. Replace the pillars over the dowels and ensure they are all facing the same way.

Dowelling a cake using hollow pillars

SOLID PLASTER PILLARS

After dowelling, solid plaster pillars should only just sit on the surface of the cake. This ensures that when weight is applied from upper tiers, the pillars are not forced deeper into the surface of the cake, which may then mark or crack the icing. Cutting the dowels 1mm or 2mm longer than actually required allows for compression.

1. Mark the pillar/dowel positions on your cake carefully.

2. Insert the dowel vertically (as for hollow pillars).

3. Mark the dowel 1mm or 2mm above the cake.

4. Remove the dowels, cut to length and re-insert. Place the solid pillars on top and, if necessary, adjust the length of the dowels so that the pillars only just touch the surface of the cake.

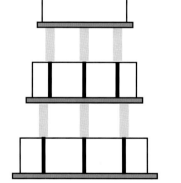

Dowelling a cake using solid plaster pillars

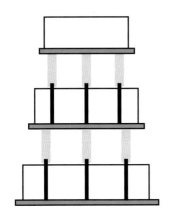

SOLID PLASTER PILLARS WITH DOWEL HOLES

Some plaster pillars have a pre-drilled dowel hole in the base, making them easy to use. The dowel fits neatly in the pre-drilled hole and provides extra stability as the pillar is also anchored to the dowel. (If you are using solid plaster pillars, you can make a small hole in the base using a scalpel or sharp craft knife if you prefer to work this way.)

1. Insert the dowel into the pre-drilled hole and measure the depth of the hole (e.g. 10mm).

2. Remove the dowel and insert it into the cake as before. Mark the dowel 11mm or 12mm (i.e. the depth of the hole plus 1 or 2mm extra) above the level of the cake and cut to the required length.

3. Re-insert the dowel and place the pillar onto the dowel. Adjust the length of the dowel if necessary so that the pillar only just touches the surface of the cake.

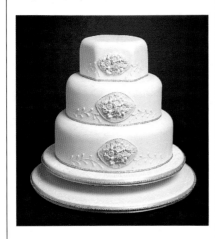

Dowelling a cake using solid plaster pillars with pre-drilled dowel holes

STACKED CAKES

A stacked cake is normally dowelled to avoid the possibility of the upper tiers sinking into the icing of the lower tiers. In this case, the dowels are usually inserted into the cake in exactly the same place as where pillars would be positioned. Think about the overall weight on the lower tiers: a small-sized, two-tier stacked cake may not require dowelling, providing the lower tier is made of a firm cake base. When the lower tiers are made of a chocolate or sponge type cake base, they may compress with the weight of the upper tier, so are best dowelled to avoid any problems.

1. Mark the dowel positions carefully on the cake (see Chapter 5).

2. Insert the dowels into the cake vertically and mark them 1 or 2mm above the level of the cake.

3. Remove the dowels, cut to the required length and re-insert into the cake.

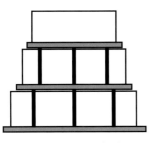

Dowelling a stacked cake

4. Place the upper tier onto the lower tier. The cake board of the upper tier should rest on the dowels and not on the cake. The 1mm gap between the cake and the cake board of the upper tier is virtually unnoticeable and is normally covered by decoration.

SAFETY AND HYGIENE

For safety, it is important to ensure that the person cutting the cake is fully aware that dowels have been used and are present in the cake. (For further details, see Chapter 12 - Looking at Safety and Hygiene.) It is for this reason that I have suggested that when dowels are used in cakes, they are not cut absolutely level, or hidden just beneath the surface of the cake.

Many hotels use electric knives to cut cakes, and if the dowels are hidden or obscured, there is the possibility that the dowels could be cut up with the cake. It's always best be on the safe side!

Remember also that when dowels are being inserted into cakes, every care must be taken to ensure everything is as hygienic as possible. To avoid contamination, I tend not to dowel any of my cakes until needed.

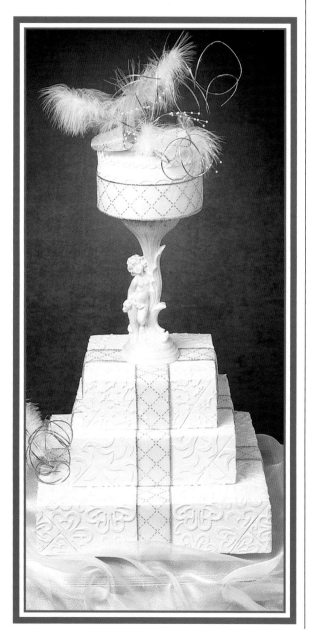

CHOOSING & USING CAKE BOARDS

Cake board is a general term used to describe cake cards, cake boards and cake drums: each one of these will have its own particular advantages for use. Each type of 'cake board' comes in a variety of shapes and sizes, which we will discuss in this chapter. However, always remember that you can make your own boards and cut them to the exact shape and size required, so the choice of board shapes and sizes is not just limited to those in the shops. Let's take a look at just what is available.

CAKE BOARDS

Cake boards are roughly 3$\frac{1}{2}$ - 4mm thick and are available in a strong, heavy-duty, covered cardboard, or a covered wood. The benefit of the wood-covered boards is their rigidity and strength. They will bear a heavier weight than the cardboard type and are also ideal for stacked cakes with dowelling support inserts as the dowels rest against the rigid cake boards and will not puncture through. The cardboard type will still take a decorated cake, but if the weight is too great the board will bend. I would not suggest using these for royal iced cakes as the movement in them can cause the icing to crack. Cake boards are available in the most frequently used shapes and sizes in silver, gold and seasonal patterns.

Actual thickness of cake board

CAKE CARDS

Cake cards are made from a covered lightweight cardboard, in single or double thickness. They are often used for lighter sponge type cakes, gâteaux, desserts and flans where strength is not required. They will not take any great weight. Cake cards are available in a limited range of shapes, but with a wide choice of sizes. Silver, gold and seasonal patterns are available.

Actual thickness of cake card

CAKE DRUMS

These are the most popular type of board for wedding and celebration cakes. Made from strengthened card, they are approximately 12mm thick and are strong and rigid. They are available in nearly all shapes and sizes, often in gold and silver.

Actual thickness of cake drum

BEVELLED EDGE CAKE DRUMS

The perimeter of these drums is chamfered, creating a gradual sloping edge. As with other board types, they come ready covered in either silver or gold foil. They provide a very elegant alternative to a plain cake board. Whilst not available in a wide range of shapes, a good selection of sizes is offered.

HINTS AND TIPS FOR USING BOARDS

- Boards do not have to be the same shape as the cake. A round cake on a square board could give you extra board space for decoration, for instance, or a round or square cake can be complemented with a hexagonal or octagonal board.

- If your design includes run-out collar work, make sure you order large enough boards so that the work does not extend beyond the board. Some board shapes are not offered in a wide size range, so take this into account when you are planning your design. If the board size you require is not available, a good alternative is to make your own.

- The design of your cake will often dictate the board type you choose. Nearly all wedding and celebration cakes need the strong, firm drums which will support the weight of the finished cake without movement. Cake drums are certainly the most rigid, but with larger sizes, even these may be susceptible to slight movement which may spoil or break some decorations, especially filigree, lace and extension work. One of the easiest and most certain ways to eliminate this risk of breakage is to make your own board from 12mm or 15mm MDF (Medium Density Fibreboard), as described right.

MAKING YOUR OWN BOARDS

You can tailor your boards to your specific needs by simply cutting down cake drums, boards or cards, or by cutting and using MDF. Ensure that whatever board you are using is completely covered with food grade covering paper (available from sugarcraft shops or via mail order). The edges can be covered with either food grade paper or ribbon.

MDF

MDF is an inexpensive fibreboard which is readily available at DIY stores (it is more commonly used for making kitchen units, cupboards, shelving and partitions). It is smooth, very strong, cuts easily and in the thicknesses mentioned, is extremely rigid. Even with a 51cm/20" square, it provides excellent support. Many DIY stores will cut it for you, or it is simple to cut at home using a hand saw or an electric jigsaw. (Please ensure that proper safety precautions are observed when using electric power tools and hand saws. Always refer to the manufacturer's guide.) The MDF is then placed beneath the bottom cake drum. It can be cut to exactly the same size, or just 2.5cm/1" or so smaller to act as a plinth (making it easier to pick up the cake). Alternatively, it can be cut larger and decorated to provide a platform for the bottom drum and the edges can be ribboned or decorated in the same way. Always remember that MDF is not food grade, so make sure it is completely covered in food grade paper before use.

Cake Drum
MDF

Cake Drum
MDF

Cake Drum
MDF

ECORATING AND USING CAKE BOARDS

- Cakes should be placed directly onto a cake board which is covered in food grade paper. There should be no sugarpaste or royal icing under the cake as the moisture from the cake can soften sugarpaste or royal icing. The icing then becomes sticky and, given the right conditions, i.e. warmth and time, mould can start to grow (similar to that on jam) which can give the cake a bitter taste and, when the cake is cut into, the mould may be visible.

- Cake boards need not just be functional but can also be fun! Think about using them to follow through the design, for example, copying a brushed embroidery design from the cake and transferring it onto the cake board covered in sugarpaste or royal icing, or piping a design onto the board to match any decorative work on the cake. You could use two boards underneath the bottom tier with the lower one in a larger size and covered in fabric a shade darker than the decorations. If there is spare bridal or bridesmaid fabric, this could also be used.

- To stick fabric to a cake board, use either a spray adhesive or a fabric glue which dries clear. To stick food grade covering paper to the board, use a non-toxic glue or glue stick. Do make certain the glue will not come into contact with any edible components.

- Textured rolling pins in superb designs turn

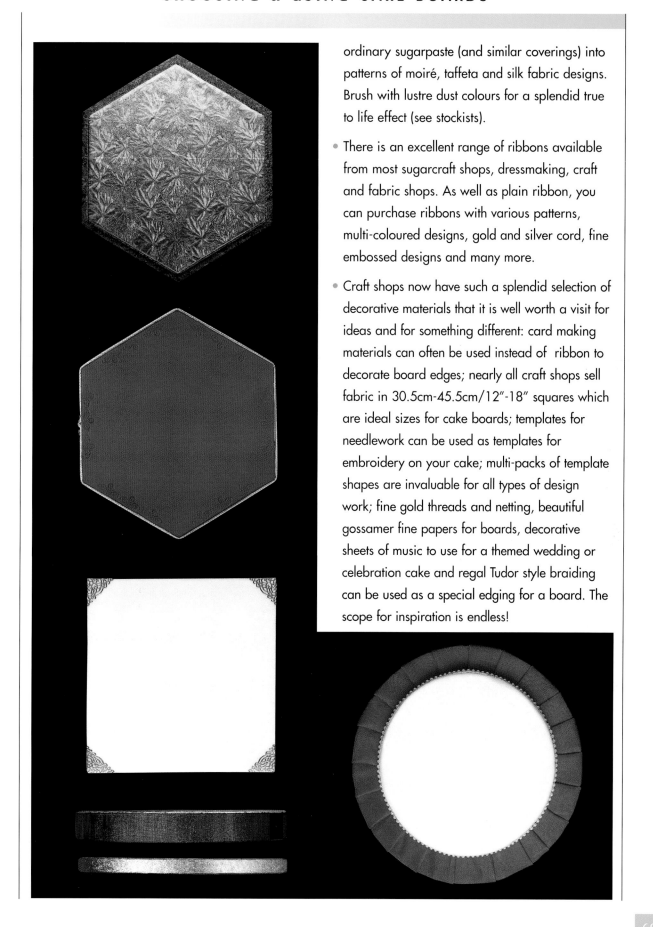

ordinary sugarpaste (and similar coverings) into patterns of moiré, taffeta and silk fabric designs. Brush with lustre dust colours for a splendid true to life effect (see stockists).

• There is an excellent range of ribbons available from most sugarcraft shops, dressmaking, craft and fabric shops. As well as plain ribbon, you can purchase ribbons with various patterns, multi-coloured designs, gold and silver cord, fine embossed designs and many more.

• Craft shops now have such a splendid selection of decorative materials that it is well worth a visit for ideas and for something different: card making materials can often be used instead of ribbon to decorate board edges; nearly all craft shops sell fabric in 30.5cm-45.5cm/12"-18" squares which are ideal sizes for cake boards; templates for needlework can be used as templates for embroidery on your cake; multi-packs of template shapes are invaluable for all types of design work; fine gold threads and netting, beautiful gossamer fine papers for boards, decorative sheets of music to use for a themed wedding or celebration cake and regal Tudor style braiding can be used as a special edging for a board. The scope for inspiration is endless!

To create space between the board and the cake a piece of oasis can be used. Here, I have used bear grass to enhance the design.

Covering A Cake Board

Whatever type of cake board you are using, it will always look better if it is covered than if left as it is. It is almost always the case that the board is covered in the same medium as the cake (for design purposes).

SUGARPASTE AND SIMILAR ROLL-OUT COVERINGS

METHOD 1

1. Roll out the sugarpaste thinly on a non-stick board, making it large enough to cover the whole of the cake board.

2. Lightly moisten the edges of the cake board with cooled boiled water using a brush.

3. Pick up the sugarpaste and lay it over the cake board. Smooth the surface using smoothers and trim the edges neatly.

4. Draw round the cake (which should already be covered) on greaseproof paper, or use a cake tin to make a template of the cake shape, cut out and transfer the greaseproof template to the centre of the covered board.

5. Using a sharp knife, cut round the template and remove the central piece of sugarpaste beneath.

6. Place the cake directly onto the cake board. The visible part of the cake board remains decorated with sugarpaste.

METHOD 2

1. Place the decorated cake onto the cake board.

2. Roll a piece of sugarpaste on a non-stick board long enough and wide enough to go round and cover the perimeter of the cake board. Smooth carefully and cut along one long edge neatly.

3. Lightly moisten the cake board around the cake with cooled boiled water.

4. Pick up the strip of sugarpaste and, beginning at the back of the cake, lay the strip of sugarpaste around the perimeter of the board, making sure the cut edge sits neatly against the bottom of the cake. Continue until the strip overlaps slightly with the starting point.

5. Cut straight through both layers of the strip and discard the excess pieces of paste. You should have two cleanly cut edges which will meet perfectly.

ROYAL ICING

METHOD 1

1. The cake needs to have had the final layer of flat icing applied before the board can be covered. Place the cake on the board onto a turntable.

2. Use a palette knife to spread royal icing onto the board. Hold the palette knife horizontally so it rests on the icing on the board at the back of the cake. Keeping the knife in this position, completely rotate the turntable in one continuous movement and carefully bring the palette knife away with as little of a take-off mark as possible.

3. Smooth the very outer edge with the palette knife and leave to dry.

METHOD 2

1. Place the iced cake on the board.

2. Pipe a line of royal icing around the very edge of the cake board using a number 1 tube.

3. Using run-out consistency royal icing, flood in the board between the piped outline and the cake base. Leave to dry.

HOW TO USE
COLOUR
SUCCESSFULLY

Colour is a very powerful tool and an exciting element in cake design. It can reflect mood and atmosphere, it can suggest warmth and coldness, it can be stimulating or calming, and express feelings of tranquillity or vitality. Colour has the power to do all of this and we can harness this power and use it with great effect in cake decorating.

In this chapter we will look at how colour is made up, how to mix and choose colours that go well together, how to use strong and vibrant colours, and using edible metallic colours. The second part of the chapter deals with colouring icings and coverings and choosing the most suitable kind of colourings. At the end of this chapter you will find a table which lists the colours of various flowers, leaves and berries to enable you to select those flowers or leaves which are most appropriate to your colour scheme.

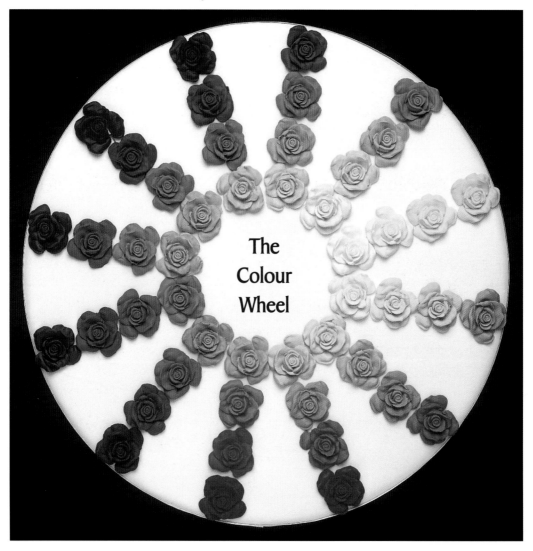

The Colour Wheel

How Colour Is Made Up

All colours derive from the three primary colours, **RED**, **BLUE** and YELLOW. These are strong colours and cannot be created by mixing any other colours together.

The secondary colours and all variations in-between are made by mixing two or more of the primary colours together. The secondary colours are as follows:-

RED + BLUE = PURPLE

BLUE + YELLOW = GREEN

YELLOW + RED = ORANGE

White added to a colour gives a tint, e.g. pink is a tint of red.

Black added to a colour gives a shade, e.g. burgundy is a shade of red.

Black and white (grey) added to a colour gives a tone, e.g. dusky pink is a tone of red.

Food colours can be mixed together to give an infinite range of colours, shades, tints and tones. The colour scheme for any cake design should enhance and complement the design, whether there is just one main colour used or the scheme is a dramatic one.

Choosing Colour for Decoration
Base Colour

When covering a cake, the base colour will provide a background for the other colours which will be incorporated into the design, so it is important to choose a suitable one. The easiest and most versatile base colours to work with when covering a cake are white, creams and ivories. These can be used successfully with virtually any other colours and are the most popular choice for wedding cakes. Pastel base colours also work well and can be used successfully with most other colours. Strong or dark base colours used for covering cakes can limit the choice of colour you use for the decoration but can be striking.

When you are choosing the colour scheme, the finished cake should look well-finished, appealing, and edible (would you choose to eat a black, dark blue or green cake? Would the guests appreciate black or green teeth on the wedding photos?). Bear these things in mind when you are designing your cake.

COLOUR COMBINATIONS

Choosing colours that complement each other is also essential. Nature itself is the very best guide when searching for colours which go together well. Simply looking at gardens and hedgerows provides you with a mass of information! If you go past a florist's, look carefully at the flowers. A white lily, for example, is not just one colour, but is made up of whites, off-whites, ivories, creams, deep creams, lime greens, deep greens and yellow. Using just that one flower for inspiration, you can see that all those colours will blend and complement each other and provide a well-balanced colour scheme.

MONOCHROMATIC COLOUR SCHEMES

Another simple method of choosing colours that go well together is to use colours from the same 'parent', i.e. a colour combined with various shades and tints of that colour. These are called monochromatic colour schemes.

When making flower arrangements (whether the flowers are sugar, fresh or silk), green is nature's neutral colour and will bring harmony and balance to the arrangement.

Using these graded colourings will give a far more pleasing effect than decorations made from one single colour without any tints or shades. Any of the lighter base colours mentioned previously provide excellent bases for simple or more complex colour schemes.

COMPLEMENTARY COLOURS

Complementary colour schemes can also be very successful. These use colours that are opposite to each other on the colour wheel.

With a suitable base colour and careful selection, strong, bold, multi-coloured designs can look stunning, as can a rainbow of soft gentle pastel colours. If using strong colours, they should not all be vibrant and overpowering. Try to incorporate tints and shades of the stronger colours used. It is important to choose a suitable base colour before adding any complementary colours.

These are some examples of complementary colour schemes which I have found to work well:-

A   Red with green and coral, creams, aubergines and limes.

B   Purple with yellows and creams, lavenders, greens.

C   Orange with dark green and lemons, ambers, apricots, russets, mid greens and limes.

A   **B**   **C**

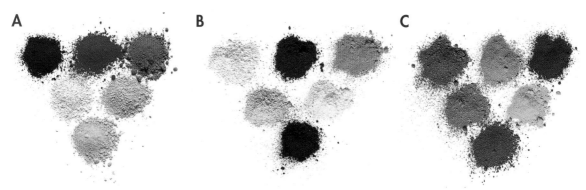

HARMONIOUS COLOURS

Harmonious colour schemes use a mix of between three and six colours which are next to each other on the colour wheel. The choice of colours used may need more consideration than other colour schemes, but the overall effect can look stunning. Use tints and shades rather than mixing too many strong colours. I always think of anemones as harmonious, the strong purples, reds and blues, but to use only these strong dark colours on a cake design can be overpowering. The overall colour scheme is softened by using tints and shades of the same colour and adding pale silvery greys, then blending in lime greens, mid greens and darker greens (nature's neutral colour).

Colour scheme suggestions:-

A   Lavenders, lilacs, dusky pinks with greys and creams.

B   Yellows, limes, greens, creams and marigolds.

C   Reds, oranges, yellows and deep ambers.

D   Blues, greens, yellows and tints.

E   Terracotta, peaches, apricots and amber.

F   Blues, purples, red and tints.

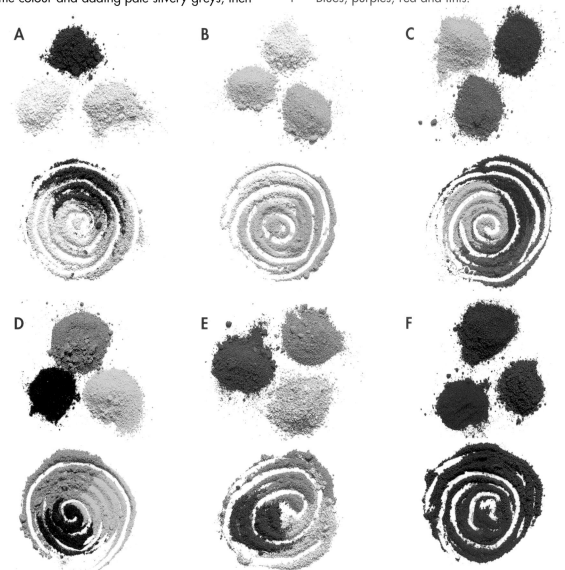

GOLD, SILVER AND OTHER METALLIC COLOURS

Gold and silver are becoming increasingly popular on celebration cakes. They can add a touch of richness and depth to a design, co-ordinate colourings on fabrics, and provide endless opportunities for novelty designs. The advent of edible gold and other metallic effect colours opens up exciting avenues in cake design and is particularly useful where decorations are to be placed directly onto a cake.

Metallic colours can serve a number of purposes: they can be incorporated into flowers, used to embellish and gild a decorative piece, or to highlight monograms and plaques, for example.

To 'paint' decorations (e.g. sugar leaves) a metallic colour, you can either use edible food paint or a mixture of edible metallic food dust and either isopropyl alcohol (IPA) or clear spirit (e.g. vodka). This gives an intense colour and allows you to brush the colour onto specific areas.

Metallic dust food colour can also be used to add colour to sugar work. For a subtle colour, brush the dust directly onto sugar work using a dry brush: this works well for adding silver tips to lace work or leaves. For a more intense, solid colour, apply Gildesol (see stockists on page 144) to the sugar work before brushing on the dust colour. The Gildesol adheres the dust to the sugar and can either be brushed on or spread onto a non-stick board, onto which paste is then rolled. This gives an even coverage and is useful for covering large surface areas. For a truly realistic effect, 'burnish' the gilded item using a soft, dry paintbrush. Plaster pillars can also be highlighted or gilded with these

colours. A visit to your sugarcraft shop is well worthwhile to see the choices available.

Metallic colours work particularly well with modellling chocolate. Decorations made from moulds and hand-modelled pieces can be given a gold, silver, pearl or copper finish which can really enhance a design.

Gold and silver leaf are also available from sugarcraft shops and give a unique metallic effect. Unlike edible metallic paint or dust, fine pieces of gold or silver leaf must be transferred to the cake very carefully using tweezers or a paintbrush. The leaf is adhered to sugar work using sugar glue, gum arabic solution or confectioners' glaze. Make sure you only apply the adhesive to the area you wish to cover and you may find it necessary to mask off the surrounding area with greaseproof paper. If you have never used gold or silver leaf before, it is worth practising on a spare piece of paste first as it can be quite tricky to use. Avoid using your fingers to pick up the leaf as it is extremely fine. It is also easily wasted, so do take extra care when handling it. Gold and silver leaf is available from sugarcraft shops and can be used to decorate most sugar work, for example, sugarpaste and sugar flowers, and is also ideal for use on chocolates, cakes and desserts. (Although gold and silver leaf is edible, it is not always prepared in food grade conditions, so check the labelling before you buy to ensure you know exactly what you are using.)

Always be certain the metallic effect colours you are using are edible.

EDIBLE FOOD COLOURS IN SUGAR

Regulations now control the amount of edible food colour that can be added to sugars. This is particularly important for the cake decorator as most of the ingredients we use are sugar. The use of colours in cake decoration is controlled by The Colours in Food Regulations 1995 (SI number 1995/3124, as amended by SI number 2000/481 and SI number 2001/3442). Under these regulations, there are a number of colours permitted for use in cake decorations. The Regulations also provide the maximum levels at which each colour is allowed. A copy can be obtained from the Stationery Office Publications Centre, P. O. Box 276, London SW8 5DT. Telephone +44 (0) 870 600 5522, fax orders on +44 (0) 870 600 5533.

COLOURED ICINGS AND COVERINGS

ICINGS

The choice of colour scheme for the decoration of a cake is often dependent upon the fabrics, flowers or theme of a celebration. Food colours can be blended and mixed to create an almost infinite range of colour choice for the cake decorator which allows you to match, co-ordinate or complement the chosen colours with little or no effort.

Choosing the colour of the cake covering (base colour) is the starting point followed by any other decorative work. If you are matching the icing to bridal or other fabrics, a swatch of material is of great help. Refer to the colour wheel to select the colours you will need to mix together to match your chosen colour scheme.

READY-COLOURED SUGARPASTE

Sugarpaste is available in a wide range of ready-made colours including white, ivory, pastel shades and stronger colours. You can use the colours as they are or mix them. The most popular choice for wedding and celebration cakes is still ivory or white followed by pastel shades with the stronger colours being used less frequently. The ready-made colours are extremely useful as you can be sure of uniformity and consistency of colour.

MIXING READY-COLOURED SUGARPASTE

This is a very simple and reliable way of ensuring a consistent colour match and is especially useful

where larger quantities of sugarpaste are required. Decide on the shade you require, for example, 75% white sugarpaste mixed with 25% ivory sugarpaste will give a very pale ivory/off white colour, then record the amounts used to obtain your chosen shade to ensure any further mixes will be consistent in colour. The same method is applied when mixing any of the ready-coloured sugarpastes.

COLOURING YOUR OWN SUGARPASTE

Paste food colours can be added to white or ready-coloured sugarpaste to create a whole spectrum of colour. Avoid using large quantities of liquid colour as this can alter the consistency of the sugarpaste and make it difficult to roll out.

Dust (powder) colour can be used, but thorough mixing to avoid streaking is necessary and the depth of colour may be difficult to achieve if a stronger colour is required. A range of extra strength colours is available in paste and powder form (see stockists). Do bear in mind that coloured sugarpaste often dries slightly darker.

When adding paste colour to sugarpaste, use a cocktail stick and add small amounts of colour at a time. You can always add more, but you cannot take it out! Colour a small sample amount to begin with, and when the required colour is obtained, use that as a guide for the remainder, ensuring that you colour enough paste to cover the whole cake (and boards). Always check the colour of the paste in daylight.

After mixing, sugarpaste benefits from resting (covering and leaving overnight, or at least for a few hours). This reduces the possibility of air bubbles when rolling out and allows any pigment to be fully absorbed into the paste. Make sure you keep the sugarpaste covered when not in use.

COLOURING ROYAL ICING

Royal icing is made up as white then coloured as required. As with sugarpaste, it is wise to colour enough icing to complete your work as subsequent batches may not be exactly the same shade. The best type of colouring to use for royal icing is liquid or dust (powder). This is because most paste colours contain glycerine and/or glucose, which attract moisture and can adversely affect royal icing work, particularly with strong colouring. Run-out work and lace work may become crumbly and not set properly, although using a tiny amount will not have any significant affect.

If you need a deep coloured royal icing for decorative work, use liquid colour and dust colour combined. There is a limited range of extra strength powder colours available, so ensure the colour you choose is feasible before starting. When adding liquid colour to royal icing, use a dropper to control the amount being added. As well as avoiding the problem of adding too much colour (and subsequently altering the consistency of the icing), this method allows you to keep an accurate record of the amount of colour used if further batches of icing are required.

Royal icing made up with egg white may have a slightly yellow tinge. To obtain the pristine white associated with royal icing, a tiny amount of blue food colouring can be added. Royal icing made up with a fortified albumen produces a good white colour and the addition of blue is normally unnecessary.

Once the icing has been coloured, leave it to rest

to allow the pigment to fully develop and disperse. Mix again before use to ensure completely even colouring.

For any run-out work, lace or filigree work there should be no glycerine in the icing as this retards the setting.

COLOURING BUTTERCREAM

Buttercream takes colour easily using paste or powder colours. Again, excessive amounts of liquid colour can alter the consistency of the buttercream, so either make it stiffer to begin with or use a paste or powder colour. Remember that buttercream is not white to start with but cream, so add colours accordingly.

Different types of food colour will each have their own advantages for different applications. A guide to using food colours is given on page 131.

FLOWERS IN COLOUR SCHEMES

WHITE/CREAM		REDS
Alstromeria	Gerbera	Anemone
Anthurium	Honeysuckle	Bouvardia
Aster	Hyacinth Pip	Calla Lily
Bouvardia	Hydrangea	Carnation
Bridal Gladiolus	Iris	Chrysanthemum
Campanula	Lily	Gerbera
Chincherinchee	Lily-of-the-Valley	Gloriosa Lily
Chrysanthemum	Narcissus	Leucadendron
Cymbidium Orchid	Peony	Lily
Daffodil	Phalaenopsis orchid	Peony
Daisy	Poinsettia	Poinsettia
Delphinium	Rose	Poppy
Dendrobium Orchid	Stephanotis	Protea
Eustoma	Sweet Pea	Rose
Freesia		Tulip

PINKS

Alstromeria	Hydrangea
Anemone	Lavetera
Anthurium	Lily
Bouvardia	Nerine
Camellia	Peony
Carnation	Protea
Chrysanthemum	Ranunculus
Eustoma	Rose
Freesia	Sweet Pea
Gerbera	Tulip
Hyacinth Pip	

YELLOWS

Alstromeria
Buttercup
Carnation
Chrysanthemum
Cymbidium Orchid
Daffodil
Euphorbia
Forsythia
Freesia
Gerbera
Honeysuckle
Ixia
Jasmine
Lily
Mimosa
Narcissus
Poppy
Primrose
Ranunculus
Rose
Sunflower
Sweet Pea
Tulip

ORANGES

Alstromeria
Carnation
Chrysanthemum
Crocosmia
Cymbidium Orchid
Gerbera
Lily
Marigold
Nasturtium
Rose
Strelitzia

PEACHES/TERRACOTTA

Alstromeria
Azalea
Carnation
Chrysanthemum
Freesia
Hypericum Berry
Lily
Ranunculus
Rose
Sweet Pea

GREENS

Anthurium
Calla Lily
Cymbidium Orchid
Euphorbia
Hops
Hydrangea
Molucella

PURPLES

Aster	Heather
Campanula	Rose
Dendrobium Orchid	Sweet Pea
Eustoma	Thistle
Freesia	Tulip

BLUES

Agapanthus

Borage

Cornflower

Delphinium

Eryngium

Grape Hyacinth

Hyacinth Pips

Hydrangea

Iris

Scabious

VIOLETS

Anemone

Aster

Eustoma

Heather

Hydrangea

Rose

Sweet Pea

REDS

Leucadendron

Maples

Photinia

Quercus

Rose Leaves

LEAVES

The colour of the leaves you use can also be incorporated into the colour scheme.

BOTTLE GREEN

Bear Grass

Box

Camellia

Holly

Ivy

Laurel

Rhodedendron

Rue

Ruscus

Vibernum

GREEN/CREAM

Cornus (Dogwood)

Euonymus

Holly

Hostas

Ivy

Snow in Summer

YELLOW/GREEN

Elaeagnus

Holly

Ivy

Laurel

Oak

BLUE GREEN

Eucalyptus

Sea Holly

LIME GREEN

Euphorbia

Molucella

PURPLES

Copper Beach

Purple Sage

MID GREEN

Bear Grass

Ferns

Ivy

Maidenhair Fern

Pittisporum

Rose Leaves

SILVER GREEN

Honesty

Ornamental Grass

Rabbit's Ear

Silverweed

THE PRINCIPLES
OF DESIGN

Once final decisions have been made on such things as cake bases, shape and types of icings, you can start to think about the overall design and final presentation of the cake. In this chapter, we will look at:-

• Design sources • Personalising design • Side design ideas • Balance and proportion
• The number and size of tiers • Examples of how designs have been used successfully

By the end of this chapter, you should have all the information you need to finalise your cake details and all that will remain is for this information to be recorded and a work schedule planned.

DESIGN SOURCES

In theory, the design choices for a cake are virtually limitless. There are many books filled with beautiful cake designs which can be reconstructed or which will prompt you with ideas to create your own design. Magazines specialising purely in design ideas are available from sugarcraft shops and high street retailers. Libraries are also an excellent source for cake decorating and sugarcraft books. Spend time looking through books as these will help you formulate your own ideas. When making a wedding cake, bear in mind that a bride choosing her cake will often contribute her own ideas and thoughts.

I have frequently been approached by worried cake makers who say they are no good at design and can only copy from a book. But even by doing this you are designing: you are selecting a cake style, choosing colours, and deciding on size, so never underestimate yourself! (If the cake you are making is to be displayed for commercial purposes, check you are not infringing copyright laws by copying the cake or design. See Chapter 13 - Selling Cakes from Home for further

information.) If you are selecting a pre-designed cake you could think about altering it in some way to create a more individual style and personalise the cake, as discussed in this chapter.

If you are creating your own original design, the imagination can be triggered not just from books, but simply by a chance glimpse in a florist's window, or the designs on wallpapers, fabrics, ceramic tiles and china where colour, texture, shape and style can be inspirational.

DESIGN TIPS

- Think about the sugarcraft skills you already have and how you can use them. Of those skills, are there any areas you particularly enjoy and would like to incorporate into the design?

- Be realistic when selecting a design, whether it is from a book or you are creating one for yourself - there is certainly no reward for sleepless nights! I am a great believer that sugarcraft should be enjoyed, not endured! Always remember that even the simplest of designs, providing it is well executed and presented, can result in a beautiful cake.

- If you choose to use a skill that you have not yet mastered, allow plenty of time to practise so you feel confident when applying it to your cake.

- Before the final decision on design is made, there are a number of practicalities which should be taken into consideration, as outlined below.

IMPORTANT POINTS TO THINK ABOUT

There are a number of factors which may have an overall impact on your final design choice. These are often overlooked, so let's take a look at these first.

HAVE YOU THOUGHT ABOUT...

TRANSPORTING

- Can you lift the cake or is it too heavy?

- Will it fit into the car?

- Can you get it through the doors?

- Will the car boot be deep enough?

- Have you considered the overall size including the cake boxes?

TRAVELLING

- Will a long journey in the heat affect the cake?

- Could the type of roads cause a problem?

DISPLAYING

- Is the cake to go on a 'top table' and, if so, will the height or size of the cake hide the bride and groom?

- Will it be on a separate table?

- Will the cake be positioned in a busy place?

- Is the cake to go in a marquee and will the floor be even?

- Will summer heat/direct sunlight affect chocolate or cream in cakes?

LAST MINUTE WORK

- Is this practical?

Please note that none of these points are intended to put you off! On the contrary, they are there to help and make it easier for you: being aware of any potential pitfalls gives you the confidence to design appropriately, knowing you have fully considered the details.

TRANSPORTING

Think about the size, weight and height of the cake - be certain it will go through car doors and is not too heavy to lift. It may be necessary to ensure that decorations can be removed for transporting and re-assembled when setting up the cake.

If you have decorations on top of your cakes, make sure the boxes you use are deep enough to contain them and thus avoid damage. Extra deep boxes are readily available but make sure you order well in advance.

The overall height and weight of a stacked cake design may mean that it has to be transported in two or three sections and re-assembled on arrival.

Ensure the design is suitable for this purpose.

A large piece of sponge in the boot of a car helps to stop cakes from sliding around.

If cakes are going inside the car, remember the seats are usually angled backwards. Have some packaging or bubblewrap to wedge underneath to keep the cake boxes level. It is also a good idea to strap them in using seatbelts.

The footwell in a car is an ideal place for cakes, but make sure there is nothing on the seat above to slide off onto the cake box. It is a good idea to lay a protective covering such as a polythene sheet under the cake box to protect the cake.

TRAVELLING

Most journeys are on well maintained roads, but if you know this may not be the case, try to ensure your decorations are either well secured to the cake or are removable.

Pack the cakes and decorations carefully, using packaging round the boxes to prevent movement.

Remember that roundabouts, bends and potholes in roads are not cake friendly!

Summer heat in a car can be excessive and a potential problem if you are transporting a chocolate cake or one filled with cream. Freezer blocks placed inside the boot alongside the cake

boxes are extremely useful. For longer journeys, make sure the car can be kept cool enough to avoid the risk of bacterial growth on the cake.

Car window sign (see stockists)

DISPLAYING

If the cake is to go on the 'top table', ensure the design, size and height of the cake will not obscure the bridal couple (or other recipient). If it is going on a separate table, see if it can be placed in a quiet but prominent part of the room

and out of strong sunlight, especially if it is a chocolate or cream cake. A marquee may not have a perfectly level or stable floor! Think about a design (and presentation) that will withstand a certain degree of movement or vibration from the floor.

LAST MINUTE WORK

Allow plenty of time to complete any finishing off or re-assembly and be certain this will not clash with any other commitments you may have on the day. Could someone else do this for you?

Personalising Design

Simply co-ordinating the colours of the cake with the celebration will help personalise the cake, but there are also a number of other ways to add a personal touch.

You may find that the recipients of the cake have interesting hobbies, occupations or particular interests which could form some aspect of the original design, for example, music or sport.

If you are making a wedding cake, think about picking out part of the design from the bridal gown and incorporating this into the cake design. For example, if the fabric is patterned, can you copy this pattern, or part of it, as a brushed embroidery or piped design? If there are bows, butterflies or ribbon roses on the dress, these too could be incorporated into the cake design. If there are to be sugar flowers on the cake, incorporate some of the flowers that are in the bridal bouquet and use colours which fit with the colour scheme. Fabric swatches of bridal gowns, bridesmaids' dresses and grooms' waistcoats are very useful to match colours.

Monograms or initials can be incorporated into the top and/or side design, a particularly useful design tool for wedding cakes.

INCORPORATING THEMES INTO A DESIGN

One some occasions, weddings and other special celebrations take place at particularly notable locations, for example, a baronial hall, a castle, an exotic white sand beach (semolina makes good 'sand') or a Japanese pagoda. In such events, you may wish to capture a particular theme by incorporating it into the design of the cake - this can prove to be both inspirational and fun!

Side Design Ideas

If you intend to have a great deal of decoration on the cake, consider its position in relation to the side design (if any). Flowers trailing down the side of a cake decorated with lace and extension work could be disastrous! In this case, you could position the flowers so they are safely away from the sides of the cake, or alternatively, prepare a side design which incorporates a space for the flowers to trail without causing damage.

Ensure that any focal point on the sides of cakes - monograms for instance - are not obscured by other decorations.

These are a few side designs which show a range of styles and techniques.

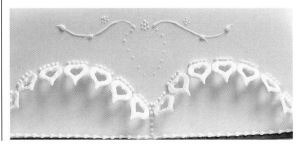 

BALANCE AND PROPORTION

A multi-tiered cake consists of cake bases built up in graduating sizes. The largest forms the bottom tier with the smallest on the top. When combining two, three, four or more tiers in a design, it is important that the tiers are graduated in such a way that they appear in proportion (in terms of depth and diameter) to all other tiers used. This would then be considered to be a well-balanced design. Let us first consider the depth of the tiers.

As the dimension of the cake reduces, the depth of the cake should also be reduced proportionately. There will always be a variation on opinion as to how deep a cake should be. The table below gives my personal preferences for the depth of cakes when baked:

CAKE SIZE:		DEPTH:	
cm	inches	cm	inches
15cm	6″	5cm - 6.5cm	$2″ - 2^1/_4″$
20cm	8″	6.5cm - 7cm	$2^1/_2″ - 2^3/_4″$
25.5cm	10″	7cm - 7.5cm	$2^3/_4″ - 3″$
28cm	11″	7cm - 7.5cm	$2^3/_4″ - 3″$

COMBINING TIER SIZES

It is generally agreed that graduations of *either* 5.0cm/2″ *or* 7.5cm/3″ between tier sizes will result in a well-balanced design. Each tier would use a cake board *either* 5.0cm/2″ *or* 7.5cm/3″ larger. By using correct graduations between tiers, you will find that no cake board is wider than the cake on the tier beneath, thus avoiding the problem of an ill-balanced cake.

If you are having trailing flowers or large floral displays, or decorations on the cake boards, the 7.5cm/3″ difference will provide more board space for you to work on. This also helps with transporting as you have more to hold!

The base tiers can often take an even larger board or even two boards for greater effect. The table on the following page gives examples of board sizes for multi-tiered cakes, showing how larger sizes can be used below the base tier.

CAKE SIZES:		BOARD SIZES:	
cm	inches	cm	inches
15cm	6″	23cm	9″
23cm	9″	30.5cm	12″
30.5cm	12″	38 or 41cm	15 or 16″

(for double boards use 38cm and 43cm/15″ and 17″)

CAKE SIZES:		BOARD SIZES:	
cm	inches	cm	inches
12.5cm	5″	20cm	8″
20cm	8″	28cm	11″
28cm	11″	35.5cm	14″
35.5cm	14″	43 or 45.5cm	17 or 18″

(for double boards use 43cm and 48cm/17″ and 19″)

CAKE SIZES:		BOARD SIZES:	
cm	inches	cm	inches
15cm	6″	20cm	8″
20cm	8″	25.5cm	10″
25.5cm	10″	30.5 or 33cm	12 or 13″

(for double boards use 33cm and 38cm/13″ and 15″)

CAKE SIZES:		BOARD SIZES:	
cm	inches	cm	inches
12.5cm	5″	18cm	7″
18cm	7″	23cm	9″
23cm	9″	28cm	11″
28cm	11″	33 or 35.5cm	13 or 14″

(for double boards use 35.5cm and 41cm/14″ and 16″)

The given sizes ensure that the cake boards of the upper tiers are not wider than the cake beneath.

This is simple for round or square cakes, but some shaped cake tins are limited in sizes and you may find they are sized as small, medium and large, so here the choice is made for you! If you are hiring tins, check to see what sizes are available and buy the boards at the same time.

If your design incorporates collars or other extensions from the cake, the board sizes must allow for the overlap of the design. Check and measure your design and adjust the size of the cake board to be used.

Two-tiered designs are more flexible in their combination of tier sizes: as you only have two tiers to consider in the overall balance and design, the lower tier can be much bigger than the upper tier if you wish. The difference between the two tiers can be 5cm, 7.5cm, 10cm/2", 3", 4" or even more, providing the finished design is balanced.

Number of Tiers

People often have a clear idea in their mind early on as to how many tiers they would like their cake to have. Some decide upon a five, six or seven (or more!) tiered design whilst others choose a single tier.

The number of tiers required is very much a personal choice and it is certainly not a problem if it is the wish to have a two-tiered cake with a large number of guests, as extra portions can be provided with a cutting cake.

On the other hand, if the cake is to have six tiers, but there will only be a few guests, then some of those tiers could simply be polystyrene dummy cakes, iced and decorated in the same way as the real cakes. Things are not always what they appear to be!

One-Tier Designs

I am often asked to make a one-tiered wedding or celebration cake, but it is sometimes difficult to make it look as special as a cake with more tiers. Naturally, the finished design to the cake will be most important, but the presentation can also substantially affect the overall appearance of your cake.

Creating Height and Impression of Size

Simply using two cake drums - one larger than the other by approximately 5cm/2" or 7.5cm/3" -

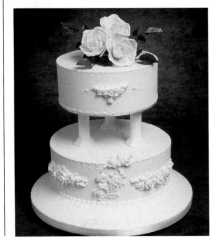

under a cake gives an impression of greater overall size and also increases the height.

Taking this one step further, creating a space between the two cake drums (by securing one or more smaller drums between the two) gives an even greater impression of size and adds height to the cake. The base board can be decorated to match the cake and then becomes a feature.

Having created new height to the cake and increased the board size, any top decoration can also be increased in size without becoming 'top heavy'.

If flowers are being used for decoration, displaying them on a candlestick, display pillar or acrylic stand gives an overall impression of greater size.

When setting up the cake for the celebration, raising it off the table slightly will also give an impression of greater stature and size. (For more details, see the following chapter.) This idea can apply to a traditional, novelty, or contemporary design.

TWO-TIER DESIGNS

The number of portions from a two-tiered cake can be more than or equal to that of just one single tier, so a two-tier design can be ideal for even small celebrations. A 28cm/11" round cake can very easily be cut and formed into a two-tier teardrop shaped cake (see template on page 33) or a large elongated octagonal cake made into a small and medium two-tier design. Another advantage of a two-tier design is the wider flexibility when combining tier sizes. With two tiers, the difference between the tier sizes can be 5cm, 7.5cm or 10cm (2", 3" or 4") or even more, providing the overall design appears well-balanced. It is also easier to combine shapes when there are only two tiers to be considered and two different cake bases can be used to account for different tastes.

CAKES WITH THREE OR MORE TIERS

For celebrations where larger numbers of guests are anticipated, multi-tiered cakes can easily provide the appropriate portions required. The cake becomes a focal point, not just because of the design and decoration but also because of its size.

BALANCE

As with all cakes, the overall finish and design should look well-balanced and in proportion. A multi-tiered cake is particularly prominent, so it becomes even more important to design the cake using a balanced combination of tier sizes. Check to be certain the shapes you are using are available in the range of sizes you need. If not, you can often cut one to the shape and size required. You may have to bake very large sized tiers in two or more sections, e.g. 40.5cm/16" square - 4 x 10cm/4" square cake bases.

STABILITY

When you are making a multi-tiered cake, consider its stability, especially if the tiers are sponge. Remember that dowelling will provide support where needed (see Chapter 6 - Dowelling Cakes).

A pillared (or similar) cake of four, five, six or more tiers needs to be very stable and thought should be given to its final display position. A very tall pillared cake displayed on a small round cake table next to a well used entrance or exit is not ideal! Be certain the cake will be set up out of harm's way and, if possible, check the location for yourself.

A design incorporating the use of a multi-tiered cake stand may provide extra stability and also dispenses the need for dowelling.

SUGAR FLOWERS ON MULTI-TIERED CAKES

Linking large trailing sugar flower displays on pillared (or similar) multi-tiered cakes is certainly feasible, but again stability needs to be considered as it is surprising just how heavy sugar flowers can be.

One large trailing floral display may be difficult to attach to a

small top tier and could cause the whole cake to become unbalanced. Think about making the floral display in three or more sections. By cleverly adjusting the odd leaf or flower, each separate section can appear to interlink with the one above and below, and it should be possible for the joins to be completely disguised. The overall look will be virtually the same as one long display. It will be easier to transport, easier to assemble, easier for cutting and much more stable.

MULTI-TIERED DESIGNS USING CAKES AND DUMMIES

I am often asked to make a six or more tiered cake, but as the number of portions this would give is usually well in excess of what is needed, it is acceptable to suggest that one, two or even more cake tiers be substituted for polystyrene dummies. Polystyrene cake dummies are available from sugarcraft shops and by mail order. They are available in virtually all shapes and sizes and some firms will cut to your own templates.

STACKED CAKES

Two or more tiers placed on top of each other is known as a stacked design. (Although pillars/separators are not used, it is usually a good idea to dowel stacked cakes. See Chapter 6 - Dowelling Cakes.) Unlike a pillared cake, the tiers can be kept together when transporting the cake as it has greater stability. However, remember that the cake may be extremely heavy, particularly if the tiers are rich fruit cake. Before finally assembling the cake, make sure you can lift it and get it through doors, into and out of cars. If this is difficult, design the cake so it can be reassembled in situ. Depending on the number of tiers, size and weight of the cake, it may only need to be split into two sections. Where this is the case, ensure any tiers that are to be separated are not iced or adhered together in any way.

As the tiers are so close together, choosing the correct tier sizes for a stacked cake is particularly important for it to look well proportioned and balanced. For example, 12cm, 20cm, 28cm/5",

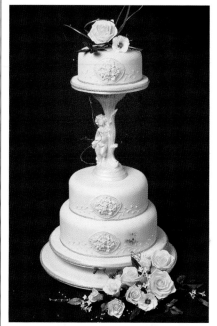

8", 11", or 15cm, 23cm, 30.5cm/6", 9", 12" are good combinations for a three-tier cake. If you are using four tiers the bottom tier could be 10cm/4" larger than the tier above. The depth of the tiers should also be calculated in relation to the size of the cake (as described on page 91). Bear in mind that with particularly unusual cake shapes (often the case with novelty cakes), the size and presentation are often dictated by the design.

PART-STACKED CAKES

These cakes often have two tiers stacked and one or more tiers on pillars (or similar). This arrangement creates more height than a fully stacked cake. Again, the tier sizes are important as well as the cake drum sizes (the cake drum should not be larger than the cake below). Part-stacked cakes allow plenty of space for decoration, especially trailing or large flower displays. The pillars, dividers or separators used can be a feature of the overall finish, especially when decorated.

USING DIFFERENT SHAPES FOR STACKED AND PART-STACKED CAKES

There is tremendous scope for design here: a combination of shapes can be very successful, adding an interesting element to the cake as a whole. The sizes of the different shapes to be used need to be considered carefully to be certain they can be positioned on top of each other without the upper tiers 'overlapping' the bottom tiers (unless this is intended, for example, with a novelty cake). For example, an 18cm/7" square cake should not be placed on a 23cm/9" round as it would overlap (the diagonal measurement of the square is over 23cm/9"). The simplest way to avoid problems is to draw your shapes on paper, cut them out and play around with them to ensure they are suitable.

Do remember that some shaped cake tins may not be available in the range of sizes of round and square tins.

KEEPING A RECORD

When you decide upon the final design, write all the details down using the tables provided (opposite), then take time to review the overall design plan. Make any necessary adjustments to ensure the completed cake will be well-balanced in size, shape, colour and design and that the final presentation will be one of which you can be justifiably proud.

Once the entire cake design has been decided upon, it helps tremendously with organisation and planning if all this information is recorded. This way, even the smallest detail is not overlooked, materials and equipment are ordered as necessary and a work schedule can be written down to help you manage your timescale.

The tables opposite are designed for you to record all the information you will need and to monitor progress. The first chart enables you to record all the design details with any ancillary information (effectively an order form). Any further information can be recorded on the reverse of the chart and kept with any working drawings of your design. The second chart enables you to list the ingredients, materials and equipment required and enables you to prepare a timeplan. Keeping all your paperwork in plastic wallets is particularly useful as they can be wiped clean, so you can refer to the information whilst baking and decorating.

You may have many months from the planning stages to the completion of the cake, whilst in some cases this can be just a few weeks, but whatever the timescale, plan realistically and allow for delays. Do not be misled into thinking you will need a shorter timescale for a sponge cake - the time taken to make sugar flowers or to prepare modelling work is the same for any kind of cake!

TIMESCALE PLANNER

Date required:	
Name:	
Address:	
Telephone numbers:	
Occasion:	

No. of tiers		Design details	
Shape(s)			
Size(s)			
Cake base(s)		Flowers	
Marzipan		Florist's details	
Filling		Board type	
Icing/covering		Pillars/separators	
Cutting cake: size and type		Stand	
Colour 1		Ribbons	
Colour 2		Swatch	
Colour 3		Knife spray	

INGREDIENTS	QUANTITY	PURCHASED	COST
Flour			
Butter			
Sugar			
Eggs			
Sultanas			
Currants			
Raisins			
Cherries			
Almonds/nuts			
Cherries			
Lemons			
Spirits			
Apricot jam			
Icing sugar			
Essences/flavourings			
Chocolate			
Cocoa powder			
Spices			
Baking parchment			
Marzipan			
Sugarpaste/covering			
Royal icing			
Other			

MATERIALS, EQUIPMENT	SIZES, QUANTITY	ORDERED	COLLECTED	COST
Boards				
Ribbons				
Pillars/dowels/pics				
Flower/modelling paste				
Wires				
Stamens				
Food colours/powders				
Tin hire				
Stand hire				
Other				

TIME SCHEDULE	START DATE	COMPLETED
Design agreed		
Baking		
Marzipanning		
Royal icing		
Sugarpasting/covering		
Flowers		
Other decoration		

DISPLAY, SET UP & PRESENTATION

The way in which a cake is finally displayed can greatly enhance and influence the overall presentation. Paying attention to even the smallest details is worthwhile. The points covered in this chapter should give you enough information to ensure that your cake looks its best on the day.

ATTENTION TO DETAIL

Once the cake is complete and assembled, check to make sure:-

- Pillars are absolutely vertical

- Ribbon around boards has not been dislodged during transporting and is even and level

- Cakes are properly aligned on pillars or stands

- The cake looks good from all angles

- Movable/removable decorations have been correctly assembled and positioned

- You have a repair kit with you - just in case!

SPARES AND REPAIRS

While most guests' handbags are filled with make-up, perfume and a handkerchief, mine is usually filled with piping bag and tube, a bag of icing and some spare ribbon! If you are attending the celebration where the cake will be displayed, I always recommend taking a 'repair kit' and a few spare sugar flowers, leaves and decorations. Invariably you will not need them, but it is a good idea to be prepared so they are there should the need arise and for peace of mind. If you are leaving the cake, take spares with you while you are setting up, then leave them with someone you know so that minor repairs can be carried out if needed.

JUST IN CASE...

Occasionally, you might need to cover up a tiny blemish that may have occurred whilst transporting, delivering or setting up the cake. This can be masked in one of the following ways:

- Pipe a few dots or a tiny design so it appears as part of the overall design.

- Sugar ladybirds can cover small

blemishes on icing, flowers, leaves and modelling work.

- Re-arrange sugar flowers, ribbon, and any other decoration if possible to cover the mark.

FINISHING TOUCHES

The cake table can be decorated as you wish: it can co-ordinate with colour and theme, be draped with greenery or overlaid with fine shimmering fabrics. However you decide to create the desired look, make sure you have the materials you require.

A cake knife placed by the side of the cake could also be decorated, not just with flowers (which can be sugar, fresh or silk) but with sprays of gold or silver wired ribbons, a tiny arrangement of berries and leaves, or a bow in a matching fabric.

PRESENTATION

Presentation is often down to personal preferences and choice, but consideration could be given to the following:-

• Try to display the cake in an area without clutter which can detract from the cake and make it look untidy

• Display in a well-lit position but not in a sunny or hot place

• Decide whether the overall appearance of the

cake would be enhanced by raising it slightly off the surface of the table. This is particularly beneficial to one and two tier cakes. If so, use extra cake boards, wooden blocks or upturned cake tins beneath the tablecloth. Take extra care when placing the cake onto the table

• If possible, set the cake up at home beforehand to see how it will look and assess if any minor adjustments need to be made.

UNUSUAL PRESENTATIONS

Weddings and celebrations taking place in particularly notable locations present excellent opportunities to display the cake in more unusual and stunning settings. On one occasion, at a Gretna Green wedding in an old blacksmiths, I used a blacksmith's anvil to display a cake. At another wedding in the Scottish Highlands, the reception was held in the most beautiful old stone built crofter's cottage complete with a superb disused inglenook fireplace. The cakes were displayed on old black cooking pots with a spinning wheel as a backdrop. More recently, I displayed a celebration cake for a market gardener on a tall upturned terracotta plant pot draped with shimmering material in greens and golds.

Grand pianos, large deep Georgian window sills, decorative arched recesses, or old oak panelled alcoves make fabulous settings for celebration

cakes; old castles often have splendid deep stone mullioned windows: cakes set up and framed within these windows look stunning. It is not always necessary to use a table! If you know the location of the venue, bear this in mind when thinking of design.

Whatever the location, from the most simple to the most exotic, take a step back and look for opportunities to give your cake the best display possible. If you can, ask a professional photographer to take a photograph of the cake in its display position. Not only will the bride and groom have a memento of the wedding cake, you can use the photograph in your portfolio if you are thinking of making cakes commercially. (Do check with the photographer if you intend to use the photograph for commercial purposes as copyright laws must be upheld.)

MAKING, BAKING
& KEEPING

The wonderful aroma is one of the pleasures of home baking, but there are many more rewards: the carefully selected ingredients and the choice of recipe cannot be compared with a factory produced cake. The high quality of any baked product is dependent upon the quality of ingredients used. So, this chapter covers:-

• The choice, quality and convenience of ingredients • Tips for successful baking

• Baking, storing and freezing cake bases

• Keeping decorated cake bases and decorations

Making & Baking

INGREDIENTS

It is certainly worthwhile buying the best ingredients available, as this will be reflected in the taste, texture and success of any cake. For example, it is often false economy to buy cheaper dried fruits as they can be gritty and lack good flavour. The following information states what to look for and why.

Currants should be small; larger sized currants tend to have tiny seeds or pips in them and will crunch when eaten. Currants are less sweet than raisins and sultanas and provide a good balance of flavour in a rich fruit cake.

Raisins should be large and plump. The best flavoured variety tend to be from the muscatel grape which is dried and often stoned by machine. Raisins are also produced from dried seedless grapes, but whilst having a very good flavour, lack the distinctive full-bodied flavour of the muscat.

Sultanas are normally produced from seedless grapes and are golden brown and very sweet. They are often called 'golden raisins'.

Sultanas, raisins and currants are sometimes dressed with a mineral oil to give them a gloss and to prevent them drying out, but this can affect the absorption of juices and moisture. It is worthwhile looking for dried fruits without the preservative. Alternatively, make sure you wash them in *cold* water before use.

Nuts can go rancid if stored for a long time, so buy as fresh as possible. For ground almonds, look for pale, finely ground nuts, especially if you are making your own almond paste as these will help produce a pale, smoother paste. If you require very finely ground nuts, whizz them in a grinder or food processor for a few seconds.

Essences and flavourings are widely available in liquid and, in some cases, powder form. A natural essence will generally give a better flavour than a synthetic version.

Spices. Powdered spices can lose some of their flavour if kept for a long time, so my advice would be to buy when needed. Vanilla pods, cinnamon sticks and whole nutmegs are more readily available from health food stores and specialist grocers than supermarkets.

Butter has a relatively long shelf life but as it is so readily available, buy as fresh as possible. Unsalted butter or the continental type butters are often used for buttercream because of their slightly creamier and more distinctive taste.

'Soft' butters are normally a blend of creams and buttermilk and spread straight from the fridge unlike traditionally made butter. However, do check the details on the packets as some are not suitable for baking.

Margarine does not impart the flavour into a cake that butter does, but it does have other advantages. Margarine is easier to cream and tends to produce a lighter-textured cake. You may, therefore, wish to consider using 75% butter and 25% margarine. Unless the recipe specifically states otherwise, avoid using very soft and oily margarines as they can alter the recipe balance. Most low fat spread alternatives are not suitable for cake making as they usually contain a high proportion of water and, again, alter the balance of the recipe.

Eggs need to be very fresh for cake making. It does not matter whether the shell is brown or white, just so long as it is fresh. Many say that free-range eggs have more flavour than battery produced eggs: my advice would simply be to

choose whichever you prefer. Hen eggs are nearly always used in cake making, although some people prefer other eggs such as goose or turkey. They will have a different flavour to a hen egg, and in some instances this is more pronounced than others. Eggs laid in dirty or contaminated places carry the risk of bacteria as egg shells are slightly porous, so be sure to buy from a reputable source. Most supermarket eggs are checked for blemishes and those with a 'Lion Mark' are guaranteed free from salmonella (a bacteria that can cause food poisoning).

Flours. Recipes state which type of flour to use to give the best results. Usually, very rich fruit cakes use plain flour, whilst Madeiras will often use plain flour with additional raising agents such as baking powder to produce a well-risen cake with a light close texture. Self-raising flour already has added raising agents blended in and is predominantly used in the making of many sponge type cakes which have an even lighter texture than that of a Madeira.

The extra light/superfine flours for sponge cakes are produced from a particular type of wheat. This makes the flour very soft and able to absorb more moisture and sugar than normal, resulting in a deliciously light textured cake.

Whichever type of flour you choose, always use a good quality brand. (Bread flours are generally not suitable for cake making as they will produce a very heavy, dense cake.)

Sugar.

With white sugar, brown sugar, unrefined sugar, soft dark brown sugar, golden sugar and more, the choice is sometimes bewildering! It is wonderful to have such a choice, especially for cake making. The soft dark brown sugars, such as molasses or rich dark brown, have a characteristic almost toffee taste and give superb colour and taste to a rich fruit cake, whilst Demerara sugar, golden sugar, unrefined granulated sugar and the lighter moist sugars offer a less pronounced taste. The fine caster sugars are excellent for sponges. Vanilla sugar is particularly useful to have in stock when making sponge type cakes which are normally flavoured with essence. To make vanilla sugar, simply place a vanilla pod (available from health food stores, most supermarkets and grocers) into an airtight jar filled with caster sugar. The flavour from the pod seeps into the sugar and the flavour in a cake when vanilla sugar has been used is excellent. It is also a brilliant ingredient in biscuits and desserts. Store sugar in an airtight container in a cool dry place away from humidity and steam.

Icing sugar

is produced by different manufacturers and often cake decorators will have a preference for one brand or the other. Icing sugar can be produced from either cane or beet sugar: cake decorators often prefer cane sugar as it is whiter and denser in nature than beet sugar, which tends to be greyer and more translucent. Most icing sugars contain an anti-caking agent to help prevent the sugars sticking together. Because icing sugar is a fine powder, it needs to be stored in an airtight container in a cool dry place, away from any moisture or steam.

Bridal icing sugar

is very much finer than ordinary icing sugar and is particularly useful if you are using fine piping tubes to pipe lace and extension work. It will give a superb finishing coat to a royal iced cake and is generally only available from sugarcraft shops. I tend to use this in preference to ordinary icing sugar. Again, store away from any moisture, humidity or steam as the powder will clog.

Chocolate

can be used to cover cakes, as a flavouring or as a filling. A high quality chocolate cake with excellent flavour depends on the use of high quality chocolate. This is widely available from many retailers including supermarkets, sugarcraft shops and mail order firms. Look for a high cocoa butter content on the packets: anything of 65% or more will produce a good flavour to cakes and cake decorations. Normally, synthetically flavoured covering/baking chocolate does not achieve the taste, quality or finish of real chocolate.

Couverture

- see Chapter 3 - Icings, Fillings and Decorative Pastes.

Cocoa Powder. Cocoa and chocolate are both produced from the cocoa bean. The bean is pulverised to a powder with most of the fats removed and is used extensively for chocolate drinks and flavouring baked goods such as puddings, cakes, biscuits and buttercream. Its powder form allows easy incorporation into recipes and produces an excellent rich chocolate taste in cakes and biscuits, puddings and desserts. In addition, the rich chocolate taste is achieved without excessive and unpalatable sweetness as cocoa powder does not have the added sugars (or fats) that are required to produce eating chocolate.

Instant cocoa powder mixes are ideal for making chocolate drinks as they often contain additional ingredients such as emulsifiers which help disperse the powder more easily in water or milk. The problem here for the cake decorator, however, is that these instant mixes frequently contain a high proportion of added sugars/sweeteners which, when used in a recipe where only pure cocoa should be used, can substantially alter the balance of the recipe. For example, 100g of cocoa powder is 100% pure cocoa powder, whereas 100g instant cocoa powder mix can be as little as 50% cocoa powder with 50% added sugars, sweeteners, thickeners and other ingredients. The result can be an oversweet cake lacking in chocolate taste, so whilst these instant mixes are ideal for drinks, where a recipe states cocoa powder, do use only cocoa powder to achieve best results.

Jam - see Chapter 3 - Icings, Fillings and Decorative Pastes.

Baking, Storing & Freezing Cakes

One of the rewards of home baking is that you can choose the recipe and make the cake to the size and depth required. If you know of any particular likes and dislikes of the guests, see if you can adjust the recipe, for example, omit peel and substitute with cherries, or omit chopped nuts and substitute dried fruit, glacé pineapple, or cherries. Recipes are carefully balanced to provide the correct mix of ingredients that will produce a cake with good texture, taste and flavour when baked, but altering a fruit cake recipe slightly and substituting as above will not adversely affect the overall result of the cake. However, chocolate and other sponge type cake bases are more sensitive, so I would generally not recommended altering the ingredients unless variations are given in the recipe.

Tips for Successful Baking

- Always preheat the oven to the correct temperature
- Line tins carefully and well (see following page)
- Ovens vary considerably, so check your

manufacturer's guide for oven temperatures, especially in the case of fan or turbo assisted ovens

- Open and close oven doors gently, do not bang them shut.

- Only check whether the cakes are baked towards the end of the suggested cooking times. Opening and closing oven doors frequently causes great fluctuations in temperature which could result in a sunken cake

- When baking rich fruit cakes, a small dish of water in the bottom of the oven helps to maintain moisture, especially for prolonged cooking times

- Carefully remove cakes from the oven when baked and cool on a wire (cooling) rack. This allows air to circulate evenly around the cake

- Measure ingredients carefully using either the metric or imperial amounts but do not mix the two

- Unless a recipe states otherwise, use ingredients, especially eggs, at room temperature. This helps prevent the cake mixture from curdling

- All cakes should be stored away from any damp or moist conditions, in a cool place and away from any direct sunlight

How to Check if a Cake is Properly Baked

- Monitor baking times and temperatures to be certain the cake has been baked for the suggested times

- A rich or semi-rich fruit cake should be firm to the touch and evenly coloured. It will have shrunk very slightly away from the sides of the tin. There should be no 'singing' noise coming from the cake as this would indicate an undercooked cake

- Sponge or Madeira cakes will be evenly coloured

when baked and, when pressed lightly, will spring back. They will have started to shrink away from the sides of the tin

- A fine hot skewer (metal kebab stick) can be inserted into the middle of a cake and removed gently. If the skewer comes out clean, with no evidence of cake mix on the skewer, the cake is cooked. (I prefer not to use this method as it leaves holes in the cake.)

Lining a Cake Tin

Lining a cake tin is one of the most important foundation steps in cake baking. A well-shaped cake will only be achieved with a well-lined tin. As well as greaseproof paper and parchment paper, you can also line tins with reusable lining material, available from sugarcraft and cook shops. This is made from a non-stick coated fabric which can be cut and used to line cake tins in the usual way, and can then be washed and reused. If you are using reusable lining material, refer to the manufacturer's instructions.

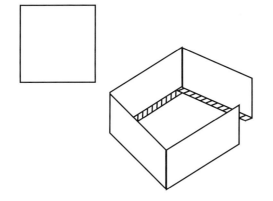

METHOD

1. Using either baking parchment, good quality greaseproof paper or reusable lining material place the cake tin on the paper and draw a pencil circle round the outside of the tin. Cut through the paper just inside the pencil mark.

2. Cut a strip of paper approximately 1.5cm/$^3/_4$" deeper than the tin and long enough to go all the way round the tin plus 4 -5cm/$1^1/_2$ - 2" extra for overlap.

3. Make a fold 1.5cm ($^3/_4$") deep along one long edge of the paper.

4. Make cuts down to the fold at an angle. This makes going round corners and curves easier and neater.

5. Very lightly grease the inside of the tin.

6. Place the strip neatly inside the tin so that the cut pieces fold in at the bottom of the tin. There should be a small overlap. Place the base template inside.

7. When lining square tins or any shapes with corners, make a definite crease on the paper lining the side of the tin to ensure a good fit.

RICH FRUIT CAKES

Preparing to bake a rich fruit cake takes longer than most other cakes, but it is well worth the effort. Most dried fruits for fruit cakes are now sold as 'ready washed' but are often coated with mineral oil or other preservatives to improve and maintain their appearance. To achieve maximum absorption and retention of moisture in your fruit, it is beneficial to remove this oil by re-washing and then thoroughly drying the fruits. They can then be soaked in spirits or fruit juices and will absorb these liquids far more readily, thus helping to make your cake as delicious as possible. They should only be washed in cold or cool water as hot would dissolve some of the sugars naturally present in the fruits and a cake poor in taste and texture would be the result. Check for any stray stones or stalks in the fruit prior to use.

Glacé cherries should be rinsed and thoroughly dried.

If there are going to be young children at the celebration and the recipe includes chopped nuts, think about substituting them with ground nuts to avoid any risk of choking (or whizz them in a food processor/blender before use).

Do make sure that all the ingredients are at room temperature before use to prevent the mixture from curdling. Tins should be fully lined using baking parchment, good quality greaseproof paper or reusable baking film as described above.

When placing the mixture into the tin, carefully smooth it to the edges and corners and make a small indent in the centre of the cake, as this helps to achieve a level top when baked.

Be certain the cake is baked all the way through and then cool on a wire (cooling) tray. When the cake is tepid, drizzle brandy (if used) over the top: at this temperature the cake will absorb the liquid well. If the cake is too hot, the brandy will simply evaporate before being absorbed into the cake. A moist cake is delicious, but remember that pouring excess liquid onto a cake can produce a soggy texture, more like a pudding than a cake.

After removing a rich fruit or semi-rich fruit cake from the oven, invert it onto a cooling tray. This will help to flatten what was the top of the cake and will give a flat surface (i.e. the 'bottom' of the cake) to work on. If your cake has a slight dome after baking, the gap around the base (once the cake has been inverted) can be filled with marzipan when decorating. For a heavily domed cake, it may be advisable to trim the top flat before inverting the cake, thus avoiding a large gap around the base.

Because rich fruit cakes are baked for a long time, a double layer of brown paper or newspaper should be wrapped round the outside of the tin prior to baking the cake. This will help to ensure the outer edges of the cake are not overcooked before the centre of the cake has been baked all the way through. Both the lining and the outer paper should be level with the top of the cake and not above as this could act like a chimney and draw the mixture up, thus creating a domed or raised top to your cake. When attaching brown paper around a tin, always secure with string - remember that sticky tape and elastic bands will melt in the oven!

Rich fruit cakes can be made many months ahead of the celebration (see timescale chart on page 127), giving the cake time to 'mature'. The sugars blend in with the other flavours in the cake and develop over a period of time. The cake will also be much easier to cut and, therefore, provide more portions.

Rich fruit cakes should be completely cold before being stored. Drizzle the brandy over the tepid cake, allow to cool completely, then wrap in a double layer of greaseproof paper or baking parchment. The cake can the be overwrapped with aluminium foil.

Do not store cakes in plastic tubs/boxes as these can cause the cakes to sweat and a mould may form. Store in a cool dry place away from sunlight. As rich fruit cakes keep for many months, it is not necessary to freeze them.

SEMI-RICH FRUIT CAKES

The dried fruits used in semi-rich fruit cakes can be washed and dried in the same way as for rich fruit cakes. Do be certain any cherries are cut, rinsed and properly dried to avoid them sinking to the bottom of the cake. When baked, the top of a semi-rich fruit cake is normally slightly domed and can be trimmed level prior to use. It is also a good idea to invert the cake onto a cooling tray (see Rich Fruit Cakes, above).

Wrap and store as for rich fruit cakes. Semi-rich fruit cakes can also be baked ahead of time and frozen. Before freezing, ensure the cake is completely cold, double wrap in greaseproof paper or baking parchment and overwrap in either cling film or aluminium foil. Thaw at room temperature and do not re-freeze.

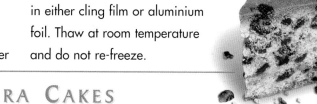

MADEIRA CAKES

Once baked, Madeira cakes, like semi-rich fruit cakes, will normally be slightly domed on the top. Again, this can be trimmed prior to use. I am often asked how far ahead a Madeira can be made: I still err on the side of caution and bake them just three days before needed. A Madeira is often better textured after three days and cuts more easily.

Wrap and store as for rich fruit cakes. Again, they can be frozen ahead of time then wrapped in a double layer of greaseproof paper and over-wrapped in cling film or aluminum foil. Freeze for no more than one month. If a Madeira cake is to be used for a novelty cake and requires cutting and shaping, it is far easier to cut the cake before it is fully defrosted as it will crumble far less.

SPONGE TYPE CAKES

When baking, sponge cakes of all types are sensitive to temperature fluctuations. Do ensure the oven is preheated to the correct temperature and avoid unnecessary opening of the oven door until baking is near completion. This will help avoid sunken, heavy textured and dense cakes. If possible, bake only one or two days before required to give maximum freshness, taste and texture.

When cold, wrap in baking parchment or greaseproof paper and overwrap with cling film or aluminum foil. Store in an airtight container. Sponge cakes can dry out quite quickly and if time is a problem, bake in advance and freeze, but once thawed, do not re-freeze. Freeze for up to one month.

CHOCOLATE CAKES

Use the best chocolate available as it will certainly be reflected in the taste of the finished cake (as descibed in Chapter 2 - Icings, Coverings and Decorative Pastes). Chocolate cakes are often quite rich, but most should still be baked only a few days before required. Again, if time is a problem, bake and freeze, but do not re-freeze. If the cake is to be covered with white or a similar pale coloured covering, keep your worktop as clear as possible from chocolate crumbs. As with all cakes, store away from any damp or moist conditions, in a cool place and away from any direct sunlight.

KEEPING DECORATED CAKES & DECORATIONS

It is tradition to keep one of the tiers of a wedding cake for a future celebration such as a first anniversary, a christening or baby naming ceremony. The only cake base suitable for long term storage is a rich fruit cake, which, unless the recipe states differently, will normally keep for approximately twelve months. Moreover, rich fruit cakes which are covered in either sugarpaste or royal icing can be kept for many months without the need for freezing.

Other decorated cake bases can be frozen for a short while, but this is not always successful and I personally would not recommend it as sugarpaste and other similar coverings collect condensation on the surface when defrosting. Once the surface has dried, this can leave marks and blemishes on the icing.

Successful storage starts with making and baking, including maintaining the strictest of hygiene standards, and is followed by accomplishing good storage conditions.

KEEPING AND STORING CAKES

- Carefully remove sugar flowers or any modelling work and store separately

- Place the cake in a strong deep cardboard box with a tight-fitting lid. Do not store in a plastic box as this can cause the cake to sweat and possibly spoil

- Use double-sided sticky tape or similar on the underside of the cake board to secure the cake to the cake box

- Plain white tissue paper can be laid gently around the cake and on the top for protection, but should not be used if it will damage delicate decorative work such as lace, extension, filigree or collar work

- Replace the lid, secure with tape and label the box

- Store in a dust-free, cool and dry environment away from sunlight

- Keep away from any moisture, i.e. dampness and humidity, as this can cause icings to stain and colours to run

- Keep away from strong smells

- Inserting cake pics into a cake may reduce the storage time of a decorated cake because the surface of the cake will have been broken. This introduces the possibility of bacteria entering the cake. If it is intended that one of the tiers will be kept, try to ensure the design does not require a flower pic to secure the decoration. Alternatively, use royal icing or a piece of sugarpaste to secure the flowers

- In the case of manufactured cakes, follow the storage instructions given

KEEPING SUGAR FLOWERS

- Carefully remove any flowers from the cake

- Line a strong deep cardboard box with bubblewrap

- Gently place the flowers inside the box and fold bubblewrap loosely over the top of the flowers, taking care not to damage them

- Replace the lid and label the box

- Store in a dry, dust-free environment

- Keep away from any humidity, moisture or dampness and keep out of sunlight

Sugar flowers may also be displayed in specially designed clear display containers. These are sometimes available from sugarcraft shops but generally need to be ordered. They are made in a very wide range of size and shape including tall elegant domes, short domes, cubes, rounds, rectangles, ovals and hexagons. Some manufacturers also offer a choice of base finishes.

A display cabinet can also house and protect sugar flowers. Place the flowers on a base such as cork, a wooden plinth or a fabric covered board and secure the flowers using fine dressmaker's pins hidden discreetly between leaves or stems. Keep the sugar flowers out of sunlight and away from any dampness as previously indicated.

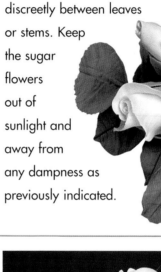

KEEPING PASTILLAGE MODELLING WORK

- Remove the modelling work from the cake and store as for sugar flowers

- It is very important to eliminate the possibility of moisture coming into contact with the modelling as it can cause warping and distortion

- Lay flat pieces on a level surface (a piece of sponge is ideal for this as it acts as a shock absorber for any accidental knocks and keeps pieces level and flat)

- Use a strong cardboard box, not a plastic one

One way of avoiding moisture spoiling your work is to keep a sachet of silica gel crystals in the same box to act as a desiccant. Remember, however, that silica gel is not edible.

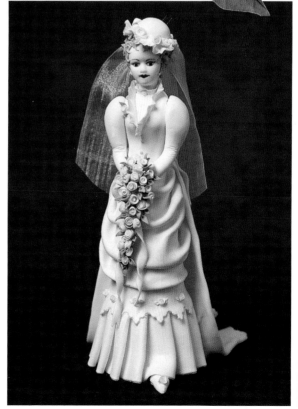

LOOKING AT SAFETY
& HYGIENE

Whether you are making a cake as a gift, as a favour, or as a commission, the strictest of hygiene standards should always be maintained when dealing with food. This chapter covers the main points which you, as a cake maker and decorator, must consider.

AREAS OF RISK

There are two main areas of risk when making and decorating cakes:

- food contamination/poisoning

- using inedible items on cakes

Personal injury and illness can be caused to the consumer through cross contamination of food and/or the use of inedible items on cakes, for which you may become liable.

Please note that the following general guidelines only cover the basic priciples of health and safety. If you would like to obtain further information, your local environmental health officer will have a wide range of booklets and is an excellent source of help.

FOOD CONTAMINATION AND POISONING

Food can become contaminated with harmful bacteria which can cause food poisoning. Not all bacteria are harmful (e.g. yeast) but harmful bacteria can cause illness and, in extreme cases, can even be fatal.

These harmful bacteria often come from raw meat and fish, as well as soil from unwashed vegetables amongst many, many other things. We ourselves are also sources of many types of bacteria which can be found in our mouths, skin, hair, nose and excreta. Without the strictest hygiene standards in place, this bacteria can be transferred to food. It is, therefore, imperative to protect against transmission of harmful bacteria from these and other sources of risk to food. The following points highlight some of the areas where risk can be reduced:

- Wash your hands before handling any food and dry them on a freshly laundered hand towel

- Thoroughly clean work surfaces before and during use, ensuring you always use a clean cloth

- Do not use knives or other utensils which have been used for raw meat, fish or vegetables

- Always wash your hands after handling raw eggs

- Only use a clean disposable dishcloth and replace frequently

- Use a freshly laundered teatowel and replace frequently

- Never smoke in food preparation areas: if you have a food business it is not permitted

- Use a separate work board kept only for sugar work

- Keep flies and all other insects away from food preparation areas. They carry millions of bacteria, so as soon as they land on food, it can become contaminated

- Keep pets out of food areas and *never* allow them onto worktops. After touching animals, wash your hands thoroughly

- Cover cuts and grazes with a brightly coloured waterproof dressing strip

- Clear up spilt food, especially sugar, as it attracts insects

BUYING AND STORING

- Check sell-by dates and buy only from a reputable source

- Keep raw and cooked foods separate when shopping and separate in the fridge: raw at the bottom, cooked at the top

- Store dry ingredients in a clean, dry cupboard above floor level

- Keep opened packets well-sealed

- Invest in a fridge thermometer and ensure the coldest part of your fridge is kept between 0°C and 5°C (32°F - 41°F).

- Don't forget to check food packaging for storage guidelines

MAKING, BAKING & DECORATING

- Don't lick your fingers while handling food or pick food from the bowl you are using - bacteria from saliva is a millionfold!

- Keep foods covered. Flies have a sweet tooth and are attracted to jams, sugars and cakes. When cooling cakes, cover with a food net

- When cooled, wrap cakes in two layers of greaseproof paper and then aluminium foil. Wrapping cakes in aluminium foil alone can cause the metal to react with the sugars in the cake

- Store cakes in a tin - plastic containers can cause sweating and encourage mould growth

- Do not use pencil on a cake: the lead from a pencil is non-toxic but non-edible

- A clean apron protects you from the food - and protects the food from you!

USING INEDIBLE ITEMS ON CAKES

Safety issues should be considered prior to the use of inedible items on cakes to avoid the risk of accidental ingestion and personal injury to the consumer. Any decorative items on a cake which are intended to be eaten must be completely edible. Ribbons, wired sugar flowers, pillars, dowels, flower pics, and plastic cake decorations are just some examples of inedible items.

Always remember these basic points:

- Never use pins

- All items coming into contact with the cake should be food grade

- Wires from sugar flowers must not come into contact with or be pushed into a cake. Flower pics must be used and should show above the cake surface. If you are using wired sprays, ensure the consumer is aware that they should not be eaten (even if the flowers are made from sugar)

- Avoid using tiny individual decorations such as artificial pearl drops. If the design warrants such tiny items for decoration, consider making them out of sugar and dusting with pearl lustre dust instead.

- Be certain any fresh flowers, berries or seed heads being used are not harmful or poisonous

INFORMING THE CONSUMER

I have used the form on page 131 for many years to be certain the people responsible for cutting the cake are aware of any items which must be removed from the cake prior to eating. I would also advise on the same form if pastillage has been used as, even though made from sugar and perfectly edible, it dries very hard. You could also use the form to advise of any particular requests there may be such as saving decorations or which cakes are to be cut. Moreover, it is often a requirement of insurance cover that attention is drawn to and acknowledgement gained of the use of any inedible items on your cake.

SELLING CAKES
FROM HOME

Once you have experienced the satisfaction of making and decorating a cake, you may feel that you would like to take a step forward and sell your cakes from home. If, like me, you are passionate about making cakes, setting up your own business can be extremely rewarding. However, do be prepared for a great deal of hard work! There are so many factors to consider and costing is an area where many people feel uncomfortable, so this chapter will guide you through the process of pricing cakes.

CALCULATING THE COST

If you are considering selling your own cakes, you will need to work out how much you should charge. We will look at calculating the costs for both non-commercial cakes, i.e. without profit, and commercial cakes, made for profit or gain as in a small business.

NON-COMMERCIAL CAKES

As a cake decorator you will invariably be asked by family and friends to make cakes. The subject of recouping the cake costs is covered here, but whether or not you do so is entirely your decision. You may wish to make the cake as a gift: a wedding cake, for example, would be a very generous gift; you may decide to make the cake in return for a favour received from a friend; you may have had many requests from various sources and feel it no longer appropriate to provide the cake without reimbursement of costs.

Whatever you decide, do try to have a clear understanding from the outset as, in the absence of a verbal agreement, it is often taken for granted that there will be no charge and it is difficult to go back at a later date to ask for costs.

Once word gets around that you make wonderful cakes, they can soon be in popular demand, so it is a good idea to decide under which circumstances there will be a charge. You could ask that the recipient provides the ingredients and materials required to make the cake, or you could suggest that, rather than charging, they could return the favour in some other way.

Alternatively, you may decide to make the cake and charge cost price. So what is the actual cost? This can be broken down into three areas:-

Cost of the ingredients

Recipe items, e.g. butter, flour, sugar eggs, spices

Fillings, e.g. buttercream, jam, chocolate

Coverings, e.g. marzipan, sugarpaste, royal icing, buttercream, chocolate

Decoration, e.g. modelling paste, sugarpaste, flower paste

Cost of cake materials

Cake boards, ribbons, pillars, dowels, boxes, wires, stamens, dusting powders and colourings, baking parchment etc.,

Cost of sundry items

Tin hire, photocopying, oven fuel costs, etc.

By adding all these individual costs together you will have the overall cost of the cake.

There are few things more rewarding than producing a beautiful cake as a treat for a family member or a close friend, but there may be a limit to the time spent or number of cakes you can make on this basis for others. If you then decide you would like to start charging more and making a profit on some (or all) of your cakes, this takes you into the realms of commercial cakes. In this case, you need to make yourself fully aware of and comply with all current relevant legislation and other regulations, including your tax and insurance position. Some of these issues are raised in the following section. Remember, however, that the highest of hygiene standards and safety issues apply in every food situation (see previous chapter).

COMMERCIAL CAKES

It is generally accepted that a commercial cake is a commission which is undertaken for profit or gain, as in a business. Before embarking on a business venture, you must comply with all relevant legislation, regulations and necessary notifications. This information can be obtained through your own research, via business courses specifically aimed at cake decorating/catering, and business support schemes such as Business Link and Enterprise Councils. The telephone numbers for these departments can be found your local telephone directory and are an excellent source of help. It is well worth the effort and, once the documentation is in place, you are ready to start.

Often, enthusiastic and skilled cake decorators decide to make cakes at home for profit and pursue the idea of running a small business. However, the pricing of cakes needs to be considered carefully. Initially, you may wish to charge the cake costs and then add on a figure per hour for your time. Providing your overheads are minimal, this should result in a profit. As your business grows, so will the overheads, so let's take a look at the components that make up the price.

Cake costs

These will be the ingredients, materials and sundry items as described earlier.

Overheads

These are costs incurred which enable you to run your business. Examples are heating and telephone bills, stationery, petrol/travel costs, national insurance (if applicable), Public and Product Liability insurance, car insurance for business use, and protective clothing. This list is not exhaustive and each business will incur different costs, but whatever expenses you incur to run your business, they need to be recorded and accounted for to enable you to price accurately.

Some of these costs are difficult to determine initially so you need to monitor your expenses carefully - no guessing! Work out how much your oven fuel costs are per hour (from your utility bill); keep a note of telephone calls for each particular commission; take into account the use of postage stamps. If you use a car for business purchases or other business use, keep a note of how many miles you travel. Keep a book in the car and record each business trip - even to the supermarket - specifically for this use. This can be used to support your claim when completing your tax return. Once you have done this a few times, you will have a good idea of the overheads you are likely to incur for each cake.

For costs such as car insurance, speak to your insurer or insurance broker. You will need to advise your insurers of your intention to use the car for business use, irrespective of how many trips you have to make, to make certain you are properly insured. The extra cost involved for minimal business use is often quite small.

Public and Product Liability insurance, whilst currently not a legal requirement, is, in my opinion, an absolute essential. Public Liability insurance covers you, for instance, should a customer injure themselves on your premises. Product Liability insurance provides cover should a person become injured or ill as a result of eating the food you have provided. The wording of all policies should be checked thoroughly to make sure they meet with your requirements. Details can be obtained from insurance companies and brokers. This may well be one of the larger annual outlays in your business to start with, though premiums vary greatly. This will be payable whether you make only a few cakes or whether you are working on a larger scale.

Once you have costed your overheads, divide the cost by the number of cakes you expect to make per year to give you the average overhead cost per cake.

Labour/time

This is the amount you will charge per hour for making and decorating a cake. The amount of experience you have and the speed at which you are able to work will be crucial factors in your hourly rate: the more skilled and adept you become, the higher your hourly charges can be.

OTHER FACTORS AFFECTING PRICING

Skill

Your skill level will dictate the standard and professionalism of your business and the quality of the finished product will bear heavily on pricing. A novice taking three times as long to produce a cake, albeit to a high standard, would undoubtedly be at a disadvantage by charging excessively for time.

Practise whenever you can and soon your speed will increase. Skills allow you to offer a wider choice to your customers, thus increasing your business opportunities. Consider training and learning additional sugarcraft skills to complement or add to those you already have.

Competitors

Have a look at other competitors' products, charges and services to give you an idea of your market value. Visiting wedding exhibitions and displays allows you to see what is already available.

Market value

Any product or service is only worth what the market in a particular location will pay. It is a fact that we are generally suspicious of a product that is 'too cheap' and should you price your cake too low you may risk losing not only a good reputation but losing out on business. Equally, price your work too high and again, you may lose business. Be sensible about pricing, take into account your location, type of customers, their needs and - an equally impor- tant factor - the standard of the finished product.

Here is a summary to help you formulate the price of your cake.

Cake costs - **ingredients, materials, sundry items**

+ Overheads - **per cake**

+ Labour - **per cake**

= Total

FINALISING COSTS

One of the major difficulties in pricing is that every cake will be different, so you will invariably be pricing cakes on an individual basis. The cost of the cake base will be constant and easily worked out; it is the design and decoration which will affect the price most of all.

Consumers often purchase celebration cakes from shops which, as they are standard with a limited choice of set designs and sizes, can be priced very easily. When a customer goes to a specialist cake decorator, they are invariably ordering a bespoke tailored/designer cake as opposed to an 'off the peg' cake.

As most cakes sold from home are made to special order, it is essential to agree on a specification for the cake. A major potential pitfall for a home cake decorator is the customer who 'only wants a simple sponge', so you willingly give a price on the information provided. The customer readily agrees,

then sends an 'oh by the way' message, 'while you've got your cake decorating equipment out, could you add a few roses and orchids with fern leaves so it will not look too plain and maybe an initial or two?' So, you can see that it is important to determine just what you are pricing - a standard or a designer cake.

Another area where misunderstandings can occur is in the cake bases. Often, people are under the impression that a sponge (a term used loosely for Madeira, Victoria or other similar cake base) will be much less expensive than a rich fruit cake. In actual fact, the difference in the cost of a basic 20cm (8") round rich fruit and the same sized Madeira is only around 10% to 15%. There may be a difference if marzipan is not being used on the Madeira, but there will be other costs for either buttercream and/or jam. The design and decoration time remain the same.

THE PRICE LIST

Formulating and preparing a price list takes a little time but is well worth the effort. Make sure the prices you charge are reviewed regularly. People often feel uncomfortable about discussing prices and a price list solves that problem. Let's take a look at the details a price list should provide.

Your list should inform the customer exactly what the price includes, for example, are the cake bases rich fruit cakes, Madeira or chocolate?

Does the price include pillars and, if so, what kind? Remember that there is a substantial difference in price between standard plastic pillars and designer plaster pillars. Does the price include delivery? Does it include sugar flowers or modelling and, if so, to what extent?

To ensure all these points are covered and there are no discrepancies, you may wish to use the following paragraph as a guide for wording:

Prices are inclusive of a hand-made spray of sugar flowers for each tier. Large bouquets and trailing floral arrangements are also available and can be quoted for according to their size.

Cakes can be coated with either sugarpaste or royal icing and include the decoration of your cake. For very extensive decorative or modelling work an additional surcharge may be incurred, which will be made clear to you during your consultations. Optional accessories to complement your requirements are also available subject to charge including alternative designer cake pillars, cake stands, decorated cake knives and delivery and set-up arrangements.

There are many alternative cake bases to choose from, including chocolate. Cutting cakes for extra portions or as an alternative choice for your guests can also be provided.

Wedding cakes tend to be more elaborate than general celebration cakes and it is more usual for you to meet with your customer to determine their requirements. Don't worry about not giving a price immediately if the cake is non-standard, either over the telephone or during a consultation - for intricate or unusual work you will often find you need time to consider the extra work involved.

Novelty wedding and celebration cakes are perhaps the hardest to price: in most cases, each cake will necessitate the need for new templates and new design work and will often involve detailed personalisation for each cake. In these cases I would not suggest giving a price without firstly determining the work involved. Take into account any research you may have to do and whether they are providing the personalisation details for you to work from.

Home cake decorators are often talented people with special skills to offer to their customers and these are complemented by delicious home-made cakes. You have a lot to offer! Persevere with your prices and do not be afraid to charge for the work you are being asked to do.

COPYRIGHT

A design which is protected by copyright may not be copied or reproduced for profit or commercial gain without the owner's prior written permission. If you are in doubt, contact the copyright owners to ensure that you are not infringing any copyright laws. This issue often crops up with novelty cakes, so do be aware of the potential problems.

HEALTH AND SAFETY LAWS

Anyone who owns, manages or works in a food business - apart from those working in primary food production such as harvesting, slaughtering or milking - must follow the Food Hygiene Regulations 1995. These cover the basic hygiene requirements which you must follow. General health and safety issues are covered in the previous chapter, but if you are working as a business from home, you will need to familiarise yourself with the Regulations. To obtain the Regulations or more details about health and safety issues, contact your local council.

Note: Throughout the book, measurements have been given in both centimetres and inches. Please note that the conversions from metric to imperial are approximate (cm usually given to the nearest 0.5cm) and you may find, when buying boards and tins, that these measurements vary slightly (boards and tins are usually sold in inches, or to the nearest 1cm).

BAKING AND COVERING TIMETABLE

CAKE BASE	BAKE	MARZIPAN	ROYAL ICE	SUGARPASTE	CREAM FILLINGS	BUTTERCREAM FILLINGS	CONSUME WITHIN
Rich fruit	Up to 3 months before celebration	Up to 4 weeks before celebration (preferably only 2 weeks)*	Up to 4 weeks before celebration (preferably only 2 weeks)**	Up to 4 weeks before celebration			12 - 15 months from baking
Semi-rich	Up to 7 days before celebration	Up to 6 days before celebration	Up to 5 days before celebration	Up to 5 days before celebration			10 days from baking
Madeira	Up to 3 days before celebration	Up to 2 days before celebration		Up to 2 days before celebration	Day before celebration	Fill up to 2 days before	7 days from baking
Victoria sponge (and similar)	Up to 2 days before celebration	Up to 1 - 2 days before celebration		Up to 1 - 2 days before celebration	Day before	Fill up to 2 days before	5 days from baking
Chocolate sponge (and similar)	Up to 3 days before celebration	Up to 2 days before celebration		Up to 2 days before celebration	Day before	Fill up to 2 days before	5 days from baking
Croquembouche (Profiteroles)	1 day before celebration				Day before		Consume on day of celebration

These general guidelines are intended to help you plan and organise your time. All cases assume correct storage conditions.

*The first layer of royal icing should be applied between 24 and 48 hours after the cake has been marzipanned.

**Glycerine added to royal icing used for coating the cake will maintain a softer cutting and eating texture, especially when the cake is decorated many weeks ahead of time (see Chapter 2).

PORTION GUIDE CHART

SIZE	ROUND, TREFOIL	SQUARE	PETAL, HEART, HEXAGON*, OCTAGON*	TEARDROP
15cm/6″	24/12	35/17	15/8	10/5
18cm/7″	35/17	47/24	24/12	
20cm/8″	47/24	60/30	35/17	25/12
23cm/9″	60/30	75/38	47/24	
25.5cm/10″	75/38	95/48	60/30	45/22
28cm/11″	95/48	118/58	75/38	
30.5cm/12″	118/58	140/70	95/48	75/32
33cm/13″	140/70	160/80	118/58	
35.5cm/14″	160/80	188/95	140/70	
38cm/15″	188/95	218/110		
40.5cm/16″	218/110			

SIZE	OVAL	SCALLOPED OVAL	LONG OCTAGON	OBLONG	DIAMOND
10 x 15cm/4 x 6″	14/7	13/6			
12.5 x 23cm/5 x 9″			38/19		
15 x 20cm/6 x 8″	34/17	30/15		45/22	
18 x 28cm/7 x 11″			68/34		
20 x 25cm/8 x 10″	60/30	56/28		77/38	
23 x 33cm/9 x 13″			108/54	112/56	
25.5 x 30.5cm/10 x 12″	96/48	90/45		115/57	
30.5 x 35.5cm/12 x 14″				160/80	
15 x 25.5cm/6 x 10″					35/17
20 x 35.5cm/8 x 14″					60/30
25.5 x 45.5cm/10 x 18″					95/48

*Point to point

Figures in italics represent Madeira/sponge cakes. All values given are based on 2.5cm (1″) square or 4 x 1.5cm (1$^1/_2$ x $^1/_2$″) pieces for rich fruit cakes, 5 x 2.5cm (2 x 1″) pieces for Madeira/sponge cakes.

If you are using a shape not included here, refer to the chart to determine the nearest shape and size to your cake. This will give you a rough guide to the number of portions the cake will yield.

QUANTITIES OF MARZIPAN, SUGARPASTE OR ROYAL ICING

The quantities in these charts are a guide for covering the top and sides of a cake

SIZE	ROUND, TREFOIL	SQUARE	PETAL	HEART	TEARDROP	HEXAGON, OCTAGON
15cm/6"	450g/1lb	570g/1^1/$_4$lb	350g/^{3}/$_4$lb	450g/1lb	350g/^{3}/$_4$lb	450g/1lb
18cm/7"	570g/1^1/$_4$lb	800g/1^3/$_4$lb		570g/1^1/$_4$lb		570g/1^1/$_4$lb
20cm/8"	800g/1^3/$_4$lb	900g/2lb	570g/1^1/$_4$lb	700g/1^1/$_2$lb	450g/1lb	700g/1^1/$_2$lb
23cm/9"	900g/2lb	1.13kg/2^1/$_2$lb		900g/2lb		900g/2lb
25.5cm/10"	1.13kg/2^1/$_2$lb	1.35kg/3lb	800g/1^3/$_4$lb	1.01kg/2^1/$_4$lb	900g/2lb	1.13kg/2^1/$_2$lb
28cm/11"	1.35kg/3lb	1.7kg/3^3/$_4$lb		1.35kg/3lb		1.35kg/3lb
30.5cm/12"	1.7kg/3^3/$_4$lb	1.81kg/4lb	1.13kg/2^1/$_2$lb	1.58kg/3^1/$_2$lb	1.35kg/3lb	1.58kg/3^1/$_2$lb
33cm/13"	1.81kg/4lb	1.92kg/4^1/$_4$lb		1.7kg/3^3/$_4$lb		1.7kg/3^3/$_4$lb
35.5cm/14"	1.92kg/4^1/$_4$lb	2.04kg/4^1/$_2$lb	1.7kg/3^3/$_4$lb	1.81kg/4lb		1.81kg/4lb

SIZE	OVAL, SCALLOPED OVAL	LONG OCTAGONAL	OBLONG	DIAMOND
10 x 15cm/4 x 6"	350g/^{3}/$_4$lb			
12.5 x 23cm/5 x 9"		800g/1^3/$_4$lb		
15 x 20cm/6 x 8"	570g/1^1/$_4$lb		800g/1^3/$_4$lb	
18 x 28cm/7 x 11"		1.13kg/2^1/$_2$lb		
20 x 25cm/8 x 10"	900g/2lb		1.13kg/2^1/$_2$lb	
23 x 33cm/9 x 13"		1.7kg/3^3/$_4$lb		
25.5 x 30.5cm/10 x 12"	1.35kg/3lb		1.7kg/3^3/$_4$lb	
15 x 25.5cm/6 x 10"				900g/2lb
20 x 35.5cm/8 x 14"				1.35kg/3lb
25.5 x 45.5cm/10 x 18"				1.8kg/4lb
30.5 x 35.5cm/12 x 14"			1.92kg/4^1/$_4$lb	

Please note these quantities are given as a guide only, to give you a good indication of the amounts of paste you will need. Remember that much will depend on the depth of your cake and the thickness of the marzipan, sugarpaste or royal icing applied. The quantities of royal icing will give approximately three thin layers with an overall depth of 0.3cm/^{1}/$_8$". Extra is required for any decoration.

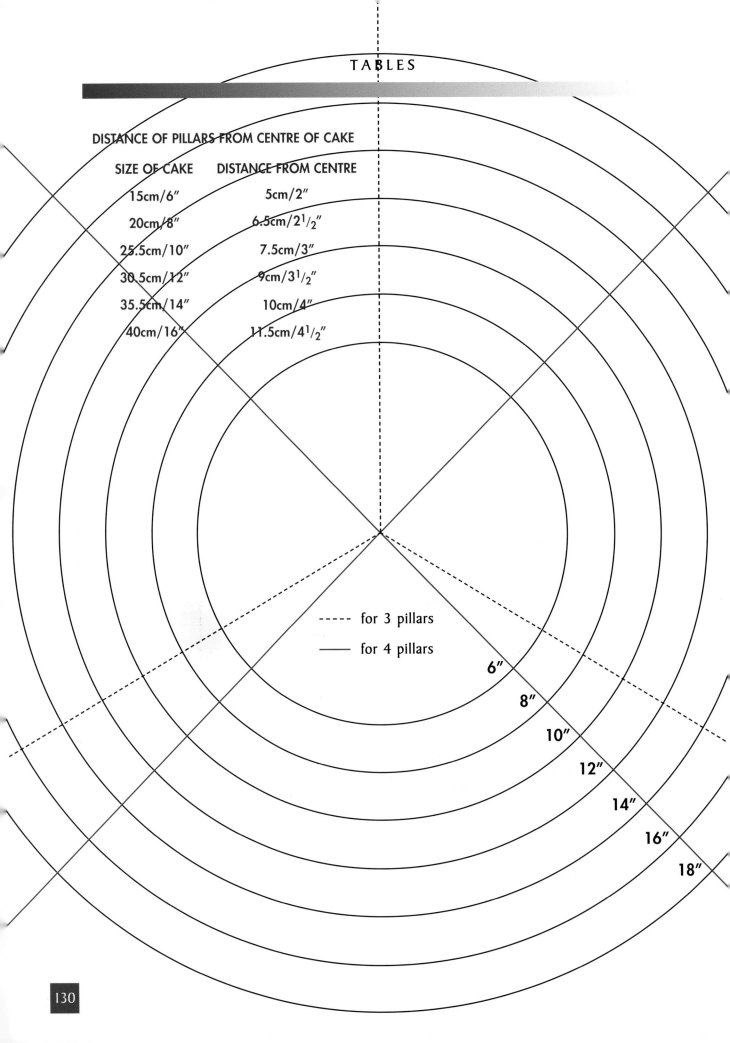

DISTANCE OF PILLARS FROM CENTRE OF CAKE

SIZE OF CAKE	DISTANCE FROM CENTRE
15cm/6″	5cm/2″
20cm/8″	6.5cm/2$\frac{1}{2}$″
25.5cm/10″	7.5cm/3″
30.5cm/12″	9cm/3$\frac{1}{2}$″
35.5cm/14″	10cm/4″
40cm/16″	11.5cm/4$\frac{1}{2}$″

----- for 3 pillars

——— for 4 pillars

6″
8″
10″
12″
14″
16″
18″

USING FOOD COLOUR

Different types of food colour can be used for different applications, that is, they work well with different types of sugar and icings. This table shows the most suitable colour for each application.

PASTE COLOURS	LIQUID COLOURS	DUST, POWDER COLOURS	LUSTRE, METALLIC COLOURS
Sugarpaste	Royal icing	Royal icing	Dusting
Buttercream	Run-out work	Lace and filigree work	Gilding
Marzipan	Lace and filigree work	Run-out work	
Flower paste	Painting	Painting	
Pastillage		Dusting	
Painting		White chocolate	

HEALTH AND SAFETY DISCLAIMER

To: . . . .

From: . . . .

Please note, for the safety of those eating the cake, I am bringing to your attention the following for which I would appreciate your acknowledgement:-

IMPORTANT INFORMATION

Please note that there are items on your cake which are not edible.

Flowers, wires, stamens ☐

Plastic flower holders (vials/pics) ☐

Pillars ☐

Dowels ☐

Ribbon ☐

Other (Specify) ☐

These must be removed for your safety and that of your guests before cutting the cake and eating it. If you are not cutting the cake yourself, please pass this information on to the person concerned.

I acknowledge receipt of the above information. Thank you

Name: . . . .

Address: . . . .

Date: . . . .

Signed: . . . .

Other instructions/information

CAKE MIX QUANTITIES

A simple way to calculate how much cake mix will be required for different sized cakes is to fill the tin size stated in the recipe with water to the level the cake mix would normally reach. Pour the water into the tin you intend to use, and note how many times the tin has to be filled. This is the number by which you will need to multiply the cake mix to achieve the quantity required.

As a quick reference, the blue table gives the approximate multiples of cake mix required for different sized cakes, based on a 20cm/8" round or square recipe. So, if you are making a 25.5cm/10" round, you need to multiply your recipe by 2. Similar shapes, such as trefoil, petal and heart can be treated in the same way as a round cake as they are similar in size. The cake mix required for different sized square cakes can be calculated in the same way, but remember that the quantity required for a 20cm/8" square is not equivalent to a 20cm/8" round.

The red tables indicate the approximate quantity of cake mix for other shapes and sizes. For example, a 28cm/11" hexagon would be treated as a 25.5cm/10" round and therefore require $2\frac{1}{2}$ times the 20cm/8" recipe.

SIZE	ROUND, TREFOIL, PETAL, HEART	SQUARE
15cm/6"	$\frac{1}{2}$	$\frac{1}{2}$
18cm/7"	$\frac{3}{4}$	$\frac{3}{4}$
20cm/8"	1	1
23cm/9"	$1\frac{1}{3}$	$1\frac{1}{3}$
25.5cm/10"	2	2
28cm/11"	$2\frac{1}{2}$	$2\frac{1}{2}$
30.5cm/12"	$3\frac{1}{4}$	$3\frac{1}{4}$
33cm/13"	4	4

SIZE	TEARDROP Treat As:	HEXAGON, OCTAGON* Treat As:
15cm/6"	10cm/4" round	12.5cm/5" round
18cm/7"		15cm/6" round
20cm/8"	15cm/6" round	18cm/7" round
23cm/9"		20cm/8" round
25.5cm/10"	20cm/8" round	23cm/9" round
28cm/11"		25.5cm/10" round
30.5cm/12"	25.5cm/10" round	28cm/11" round

SIZE	OVAL, SCALLOPED OVAL Treat As:	LONG OCTAGON Treat As:	OBLONG Treat As:	DIAMOND Treat As:
10 x 15cm/4 x 6"				
12.5 x 23cm/5 x 9"		18cm/7" square		
15 x 20cm/6 x 8"	18cm/7" round		18cm/7" square	
18 x 28cm/7 x 11"		23cm/9" square		
20 x 25cm/8 x 10"	23cm/9" round		23cm/9" square	
23 x 33cm/9 x 13"		28cm/11" square	28cm/11" square	
25.5 x 30.5cm/10 x 12"	28cm/11" round		28cm/11" square	
15 x 25.5cm/6 x 10"				15cm/6" square
20 x 35.5cm/8 x 14"				20cm/8" square
25.5 x 45.5cm/10 x 18"				25.5cm/10" square
30.5 x 35.5cm/12 x 14"			33cm/13" square	

FAVOURITE RECIPES

There are many different recipes for the same type of cake so use one you are particularly fond of and you know works well, or try one or two out beforehand. Friends or families often have favourite recipes to pass on so try one of theirs. I find one of the pleasures of cake making is to try different recipes and fillings for cakes, so do think about spending time browsing through recipe books, looking at alternatives and trying them out - it really is worthwhile.

The following recipes are simply the ones that I choose to use and are given should you like to try them, too. Please note that the oven temperatures and baking times are a guide as all ovens vary. Conversions from metric to imperial are approximate, so always use one or the other, do not mix the two. As I have gathered these recipes from a number of different sources, the weights and measurements are not always consistent with each other. However, altering the amounts of some of the ingredients would alter the recipes, and as each individual recipe works well, I have used the original values here.

RICH FRUIT CAKE

INGREDIENTS

200g/8oz butter

200g/8oz moist brown sugar

250g/10oz plain flour

4 large eggs

$^3/_4$ tsp mixed spice

250g/10oz currants *

200g/8oz sultanas *

175g/7oz raisins *

* or 625g/1lb 9oz dried mixed fruit

50g/2oz chopped almonds

75g/3oz glacé cherries

Grated rind and juice of 1 lemon

45ml/3 tbsp brandy

METHOD

1. Preheat the oven to 150°C/300°F/Gas 2.

2. Line a 20cm/8″ tin with baking parchment, then wrap brown paper round the outside of the cake tin. (This stops the metal cake tin conducting excessive heat and cooking the outer edge of the cake too quickly.) The brown paper should not come above the depth of the tin, but should be level with it.

3. Wash and dry the dried fruit. Soak overnight or for up to three days in the lemon juice and 40ml brandy.

4. Cut the cherries in halves or quarters, rinse and dry.

5. Break the eggs into a bowl and beat very lightly.

6. Cream the butter, sugar and lemon rind until light and fluffy. Add the eggs a little at a time to the creamed mixture, beating well between each addition. Continue until all the egg has been beaten in.

7. Gently fold in the flour followed by the fruit, nuts and cherries.

8. Place the mixture into the lined tin, carefully smooth it to the edges (and corners if applicable) and make a small indent in the centre of the cake, as this helps to achieve a level top when baked. Bake at 150°C/300°F/Gas 2 for one hour. After the first hour of baking, reduce the temperature to 140°C/275°F/Gas 1 and bake for a further $1^3/_4$ - $2^1/_4$ hours. (Check the cake at regular intervals towards the end of the baking time to be certain the cake is properly cooked.)

9. Remove from the oven when baked and allow to cool. When tepid, pour over the remaining brandy. Cool thoroughly, wrap in two layers of greaseproof paper (which can be overwrapped with aluminum foil) and store in a tin or a strong cardboard box with a tight fitting lid.

WHITE RICH FRUIT CAKE

INGREDIENTS

225g/8oz butter

225g/8oz caster sugar

Grated rind and juice of 1 lemon and 1 orange

4 eggs, lightly beaten

250g/9oz plain flour

100g/4oz glacé cherries (rinsed, dried and quartered or halved)

100g/4oz crystallized ginger, chopped

100g/4oz glacé pineapple, chopped

50g/2oz candied peel (orange and lemon mixed)

25g/1oz citron peel

175g/7oz sultanas

25g/1oz angelica

50g/2oz chopped walnuts

50g/2oz blanched almonds, chopped

25g/1oz hazelnuts chopped

45ml/3 tbsp brandy

This is probably my favourite cake! For those not fond of the traditional spicy rich fruit cake, the following recipe is an alternative option. It is made with glacé and crystallized fruits and nuts, and the spices are omitted. The result when baked is a cake much lighter in colour (hence the title 'white' cake) with a fresh fruity taste. Once made it will keep for three to four months if stored correctly.

METHOD

1. Preheat the oven to 180°C/350°F/Gas 4.

2. Line a round 20cm/8" baking tin and wrap a double layer of brown paper round the outside of the cake tin. The brown paper should not come above the depth of the tin, but should be level with it.

3. Cream the butter and sugar with the fruit rinds until light and fluffy. Beat in the eggs gradually, making sure the mix is well beaten between additions.

4. Gently fold in the flour, glacé fruits, sultanas, peel and nuts. Stir in the juices and brandy.

5. Place the mixture into the lined tin and bake at 180°C/350°F/Gas 4 for 30 minutes. Reduce the oven temperature to 150°C/300°F/Gas 2 and continue to bake for a further $2^1/_4$ - 3 hours, depending on your oven. Make sure the cake is properly cooked before removing from the oven and allow to cool on a cooling rack.

SEMI-RICH FRUIT CAKE

INGREDIENTS

150g/5oz butter or margarine

150g/5oz caster sugar

225g/8oz self raising flour

1tsp mixed spice

2 medium eggs, lightly beaten

130ml/$4^1/_2$ fl oz milk (at room tem perature)

350g/12oz mixed dried fruit

METHOD

1. Preheat the oven to 150°C/300°F/Gas 2.

2. Line a 20cm/8" deep baking tin, then wrap brown paper round the outside of the tin and secure.

3. Place the butter, sugar, flour, spices and 120ml of the milk into a food mixer and using a beating attachment, beat until light and fluffy (usually 2-3 minutes). Alternatively, beat by hand. If the mix is very stiff, add a little more of the remaining milk.

4. Fold the dried fruits into the mixture.

5. Place the mix into the tin and spread evenly.

6. Bake for $1^3/_4$ - $2^1/_4$ hours, depending on your oven. Check regularly towards the end of the cooking time and test the cake to be certain it is baked through.

7. Remove the cake from the oven, cool on a wire tray and store as for rich fruit cakes.

MADEIRA CAKE (ALL-IN-ONE METHOD)

INGREDIENTS

175g/6oz butter or margarine

175g/6oz caster sugar

3 medium/large eggs

225g/8oz plain flour

1$\frac{1}{2}$ level tsp baking powder

Grated rind 1 lemon

METHOD

1. Preheat the oven to 160°C/325°F/Gas 3.

2. Line an 18cm/7" round cake tin with greaseproof paper.

3. Place all the ingredients into a mixing machine and beat using a beater attachment until the mixture is light, fluffy and glossy. Alternatively, beat the mixture by hand.

4. Place the mixture into the lined tin and smooth the top.

5. Bake in the preheated oven for 1$\frac{1}{2}$ - 1$\frac{3}{4}$ hours depending on your oven.

6. Once baked, remove from the oven, cool on a wire tray then wrap in greaseproof paper and store in an airtight container (preferably not plastic).

VARIATION

For a coconut madeira, add 50g (2oz) fine desiccated coconut and 30ml (2 tablespoons) milk to the basic mix.

VICTORIA SANDWICH (ALL-IN-ONE METHOD)

INGREDIENTS

175g/6oz margarine or butter

175g/6oz caster sugar

175g/6oz self raising flour

3 medium eggs

1 level tsp baking powder

METHOD

1. Preheat the oven to 190°C/375°F/Gas 5.

2. Place all the ingredients into a mixing machine. Using the beater attachment, beat until light and fluffy.

3. Grease and line two 18cm/7" shallow sandwich tins (only the bottom of the tins needs to be lined). Divide the mixture evenly into the two tins.

4. Bake for 20 - 30 minutes depending on your oven.

5. When baked, turn out onto a wire tray to cool. Do not store until cold.

VARIATION

(Place with the other ingredients into the mixing bowl.)

Chocolate	1 heaped tablespoon cocoa + 2 tablespoons hot water. Mix together well and cool.
Vanilla	Add a few drops of pure vanilla essence.
Lemon	Add 2 teaspoons of grated lemon rind.
Coffee	Either use a few drops of coffee essence to taste or dissolve 1 teaspoon of coffee powder with a few drops of cooled boiled water. For a stronger coffee flavour increase to 2 teaspoons.

CHOCOLATE CAKE

INGREDIENTS

225g/8oz butter or margarine

225g/8oz caster sugar

225g/8oz self raising flour

4 eggs

60g/4 heaped tbsp cocoa powder

4 tbsp hot water

2 tsp baking powder

2 tsp coffee powder/granules

METHOD

1. Preheat the oven to 180°C/350°F/Gas 4.

2. Line a 20cm/8" round baking tin with greaseproof paper.

3. Blend the cocoa powder with the hot water and coffee granules.

4. Place all the ingredients into a mixing machine and beat well until light and fluffy.

5. Place the mixture into the lined baking tin and bake in the oven for 30 - 50 minutes (or until cooked, depending on your oven). The cake can also be baked in two small 18cm (7") sandwich tins (pans).

6. When baked, cool on a wire tray.

BUTTERCREAM

Please note that the choice of butter here is a personal one. I very much enjoy the rich creamy taste of the continental butters, especially the unsalted ones. They also tend to make a slightly whiter buttercream. Being very keen on healthy eating, I have tried to make a 'buttercream type filling' using low fat spreads but they do not make a good filling cream as they tend to contain a high percentage of water. The result of mine was a cross between glacé icing and custard!

If you are making cakes to sell, it is important to remember that if you describe your cakes as containing buttercream, it must only be made using butter and not a substitute fat or margarine as these can only be described as fillings or icings.

INGREDIENTS

50g/2oz butter

100g/4oz sieved icing sugar

5-10ml/1-2 tsp boiled hot water (reduce the amount of water if you are colouring the buttercream with liquid colour)

METHOD

1. Beat the butter until soft, light and almost white in colour.

2. Gradually add the icing sugar, beating well between additions.

3. Add the hot water and beat again until very light.

4. Keep covered with cling film (plastic food wrap) when not in use.

5. Store in the refrigerator, but before use, beat again.

VARIATIONS

Chocolate — Add 1 tablespoon sieved cocoa powder to the sieved icing and add a little more hot water if necessary.

Coffee — Either use coffee essence to taste or dissolve 1 tablespoon coffee powder in a few drops of boiling water and mix together. Add to taste.

Vanilla, almond, peppermint, orange, rose, butterscotch — Add a few drops of essence to taste.

Lemon, orange — Add the zest of one lemon or orange to the buttercream and beat well.

Some liqueurs, such as orange liqueur, coffee liqueur and peach schnapps, make very good flavourings but be careful not to add too much liquid or the cream will be too soft.

GANACHE

Ganache can be used for filling cakes, for piping and for making truffles or sweets. It can also be flavoured with spirits and liqueurs. For piping, allow the mix to cool and then whisk until light and similar in consistency to buttercream.

The consistency of ganache can be altered by varying the ratio of cream to chocolate: more chocolate will give a thicker mix. You can use double cream, whipping or single cream. A mix of 50% milk and 50% cream can also be used, though the taste will not be as rich. I prefer the rich taste of double cream when making ganache.

INGREDIENTS

300ml ($^1/_2$ pint) cream

500g/1lb couverture

METHOD

1. Melt the chocolate in a bain marie or in a bowl placed over a saucepan of water. Gently heat the water until the chocolate melts. (You can also make melt the chocolate and heat the cream in a microwave oven.)

2. Heat the cream to boiling point. Remove from the heat and stir in the melted chocolate. Beat or whisk until completely blended and smooth. If the mixture curdles or separates, add a little more melted chocolate and beat again.

PROFITEROLES

INGREDIENTS

250ml/9fl oz water

120g/4$^1/_2$oz margarine

150g/5oz plain flour

3 or 4 eggs, beaten

Pinch of salt

Pinch of sugar

Filling:

Whipped double cream - this can be sweet-ened with a small amount of sieved icing sugar and vanilla essence ('Chantilly cream')

This quantity of choux pastry will make approximately 15 - 30 profiteroles, depending on the size they are made.

VARIATIONS

Alternative fillings can be used such as whipped cream flavoured with orange liqueur or 50% whipped cream + 50% crème pâtissière.

METHOD

1. Preheat the oven to 220°C/425°F/Gas 7.

2. Place the water and margarine into a saucepan and bring to the boil.

3. Remove from the heat and immediately beat in the flour for a few minutes until the mixture leaves the side of the pan. Allow to cool slightly.

4. Beat the eggs into the mix a little at a time. The mixture may seem to resist the addition of the eggs but this is normal. Continue to beat and gradually the eggs will blend into the mix.

5. Place the mixture in a large piping bag with a savoy tube (large piping nozzle often used for choux pastry, piping potatoes and piping large rosettes of cream or buttercream) and pipe small balls onto a greased baking tray. When baked they will be three or four times larger in size so pipe them well away from each other.

6. Bake at 220°C/425°F/Gas 7 for 10 - 15 minutes then reduce the temperature to 190°C/375°F/Gas 5 for a further 10 - 15 minutes or until pale golden brown.

7. Remove from oven and allow to cool. I prefer to remove them from the oven, make a small slit in the base and return them to the oven to dry them out for a few minutes.

8. Once the pastry has cooled thoroughly, make a small slit in the base. Fill a piping bag with whipped cream (or your chosen filling) and fill the profiteroles.

9. Profiteroles can be dusted with icing sugar prior to serving or the tops can be dipped into melted chocolate.

Crème Pâtissière

Crème Pâtissière is a cooked sweet filling which forms the basis of many desserts. It can also be mixed with whipped double cream as a filling for profiteroles.

Ingredients

500ml/1 pint milk

100g/4oz caster sugar

Vanilla essence to taste

4 egg yolks (medium/large)

50g/2oz plain flour

Method

1. Whisk the yolks and sugar until almost white.

2. Mix in the flour.

3. Bring the milk to boiling point in a saucepan and whisk onto the yolk mix.

4. Return the mix to the saucepan and gently bring back to boiling point. Do not overboil as the mix can curdle.

5. Add essence to taste.

6. Remove from the heat and pour into a clean bowl. Place a circle of baking parchment directly on top of the mix to prevent a skin forming.

7. Cover the bowl with cling film. Cool and refrigerate.

Modelling Chocolate (Plastic Chocolate)

Modelling chocolate can be used to make decorations such as roses, leaves and small figures. It can be coloured using edible food colours and dusted with edible dust or lustre powders. To gild modelling chocolate, simply brush edible metallic powder onto the surface and burnish with a clean soft brush.

Ingredients

1 part liquid glucose to

2 parts milk, dark or white couverture

Method

Warm the chocolate and the glucose separately and then blend together. You can alter the consistency by adding more chocolate or more glucose.

Nut-free 'Marzipan'

I have frequently used this recipe to replace marzipan not just on celebration cakes, but on small cakes such as Battenburg where there has been a known allergy to nuts. In all cases it should be made certain that allergy sufferers are not allergic to any of the ingredients in the nut-free option and use a nut-free almond essence available from sugarcraft shops. (See list of suppliers for stockists.)

Ingredients

100g/4oz semolina

50g/2oz margarine

Nut-free almond essence, to taste

2 tbsp water

100g/4oz granulated sugar

Method

1. Place the margarine and the water in a saucepan and melt over a gentle heat.

2. Add the semolina and stir for a minute.

3. Stir in the sugar, then add the flavouring.

4. Cool until stiff and knead very lightly to bring all the ingredients together. Leave until cold before use.

5. To cover cakes, knead in a little icing sugar and roll out onto a non-stick board dusted with icing sugar. For a stiffer paste, slightly increase the quantity of semolina.

ALMOND PASTE

I have included this recipe for almond paste as it is easy to make. The amount given is sufficient for an 18cm/7" round cake. Increase the quantities of sugar and almonds if you prefer thicker marzipan.

INGREDIENTS

150g/5oz sieved icing sugar

150g/5oz caster sugar

300g/10oz best quality ground almonds

1 medium egg, beaten (or 2 yolks)

15ml/1 tbsp lemon juice

Almond essence to taste (if desired)

METHOD

1. Sieve the sugars together into a bowl, then add the ground almonds and mix well. Add the lemon juice to the beaten egg and mix into the sugars and almond mixture.

3. Blend all the ingredients until smooth and pliable. If the mix is very stiff, add a little more egg white or lemon juice. If the mix is too soft, add more icing sugar.

4. Do not over-knead the paste as it will become oily. This can make the paste difficult to roll out and discolour royal icing.

5. Once made, keep in a strong polythene bag in an airtight container.

HOME-MADE SUGARPASTE (KNEADED FONDANT ICING)

INGREDIENTS

450g/1lb sieved icing sugar

1 medium egg white, very lightly beaten

50g/2oz warmed liquid glucose

Flavouring of your choice, e.g. vanilla

METHOD

1. Place the icing sugar into a bowl and add the warmed glucose and egg white.

2. Knead until the paste is smooth, silky and pliable.

3. Add flavouring to taste.

4. Once made, keep in a strong polythene bag in an airtight container.

FLOWER PASTE

It is worthwhile trying out a number of different recipes to see which you prefer. I would normally choose to use a commercially-produced paste for ease and consistency. However, I am fond of this recipe as it is simple to make and does not require a heavy mixing machine. When made, the paste is stretchy, pliable and can be rolled very thinly. I tend to use icing sugar made from cane sugar rather than beet sugar.

INGREDIENTS

3 medium egg whites* (at room temperature)

570g - 625g/1lb 4oz-1lb 6oz sieved icing sugar

20g/$^3/_4$oz Tylo powder or CMC (available from sugarcraft stockists)

15g/$^1/_2$oz white vegetable fat

Cornflour (cornstarch)

*Remember that wherever fresh egg white is referred to, only guaranteed salmonella-free eggs should be used.

METHOD

(Make either by hand or with a food mixer)

1. Lightly beat the egg whites.

2. Gradually add the icing sugar, beating well between each addition until soft peak consistency is reached.

3. Add the Tylo and white fat.

4. Beat again and the mix will immediately thicken. Remove from the bowl and knead well for a few minutes on a work surface lightly dusted with cornflour (cornstarch) until the paste is soft, smooth and stretchy.

5. Put into a strong polythene bag immediately and then into an airtight container.

6. Before use, lightly grease your fingers. Pull off a small amount of flower paste and work between your fingers until smooth, stretchy and pliable. If the paste

is sticky, add a little more icing sugar or cornflour. If the paste is too stiff, add a little more egg white. Always keep spare paste covered when not in use. After use, cover as above and store in the refrigerator. Flower paste will keep for many weeks when stored correctly.

7. Colour using edible food paste colours. Adding large amounts of paste colour to flower paste can alter the consistency and result in a sticky paste that is difficult to use. To overcome this, try using the extra strength paste colours (available from sugarcraft shops).

MODELLING PASTE (1)

For modelling work where strength is not required (e.g. small plaques, swags, garrett frills, ribbons, bows and small figures), blend together equal amounts of flower paste and sugarpaste.

Increase the proportion of flower paste where more strength is required or for modelling larger figures. For larger pieces of work, use up to 75% flower paste to 25% sugarpaste.

MODELLING PASTE (2)

For an alternative simple modelling paste, blend 500g/1lb sugarpaste with 10ml/2 teaspoons of gum tragacanth. Mix

together well. Leave overnight or for a few hours before use. Always keep covered when not in use.

EDIBLE GLUE

INGREDIENTS

1 part Tylo (or carboxymethylcellulose - often referred to a CMC for short - a synthetic substitute for gum tragacanth)

30 parts water

METHOD

1. Mix 30 parts water (30 teaspoons) and 1 part Tylo/CMC (1 teaspoon) together. (Although it may be more practical to measure out 150ml of water, it is essential to be extremely accurate. I find that adding one teaspoon at a time is the most accurate method.) It will be thick and lumpy.

2. Leave for about four hours - or overnight - and the mixture will then become a clear gel.

3. Store in an airtight jar in the refrigerator. For a very thin glue, add more water. Use as required.

COLOURED CONFECTIONERS' GLAZE

I find this extremely useful when glazing leaves, berries, nuts and seed heads. It adds extra colour and for rose leaves in particular, highlights the veining on the leaves. Depending on the season, I use red coloured glaze (especially for rose leaves) greens, terracotta and ambers. I use small brush bottles, available from chemists or sugarcraft shops, and have different colours of glaze in each jar. The brush in the jar means it does not have to be cleaned each time after use!

INGREDIENTS

Confectioners' glaze

Liquid food colours

METHOD

1. Fill a small brush bottle ³/₄ full with confectioners' glaze.

2. Add a few drops of your chosen colour to the glaze. Screw on the top and shake well.

3. For a half glaze where a less pronounced shine in required, dilute the mix with isopropyl alchocol (glaze cleaner). The amount you dilute will depend on the depth of shine required, but generally speaking, 50% works well.

Albumen, fortified	Pasteurised dried egg white with bulking agents and other ingredients. Often used in the making of royal icing. Less expensive than pure dried albumen	**Cornflour**	Also known as cornstarch
		Couverture	High quality chocolate
Albumen, fresh	White of an egg	**Cutting cake**	Cake used to provide additional portions. Not normally on display or decorated but can be iced in the same style as the main cake.
Albumen, pure	Pure pasteurised dried egg white. Stronger than fortified albumen with more strength and stretch	**Divider/separator**	Used as an alternative to but in the same way as a pillar, a decorative object designed to separate the tiers of a cake.
Almond paste	A paste similar to marzipan made from a mix of ground almonds, sugar and egg	**Dowels**	Lengths of food grade rod used to provide support to tiered cakes
Angelica	Crystallised stem of the angelica plant, used in baking and as a cake decoration	**Dropper bottle**	Small bottle with top attachment which allows liquid to be extracted from the bottle and added to ingredients in single drops
Apricot glaze	A mixture of apricot jam and water/lemon juice which is boiled, sieved and used for brushing onto a cake immediately prior to applying a marzipan layer	**Dummy (polystyrene)**	Shaped polystyrene which can be decorated in the same way as a cake (not filled) to give the appearance of an additional tier to a celebration cake, used extensively for practise work
Baking parchment	Non-stick food grade paper used for lining baking tins (pans) and overwrapping food		
Baking tins	Also known as baking pans, cake tins and cake pans	**Edible gilding**	The use of edible materials to create a shiny metallic effect on sugar work as well as plaster pillars
Bridal icing sugar	Extra fine icing sugar which, when used in royal icing, produces a particularly smooth finish	**Extension work**	Finely piped lines of royal icing, normally on the sides of a cake, extending to a built out 'bridge' above the base of a cake
Bridgework	Overpiped linework used to support extension work	**Filigree**	Royal iced lacy designs piped inside an outline, made as offset pieces
Burnish	Bring to a deep shine/polish	**Flat icing**	Royal icing coating the top and sides of a cake
Buttercream	Cake filling, usually made from butter and sugar, also known as butter icing	**Flinting**	The process of royal icing breaking away from the marzipan layer beneath when cut, caused by the marzipan being left to dry out for too long before the icing is applied
Cake board	General term used to refer to cake boards, cake cards and cake drums		
Caraque	Rolls of curled chocolate		
Caster sugar	Superfine sugar	**Flood icing**	Thinned down royal icing used to flood an area inside a royal iced piped outlined design
Chantilly cream	Sweetened whipped cream, sometimes flavoured with vanilla, used for fillings and to decorate gâteaux	**Florist's tape**	Used to bind the wires of sugar flowers
		Flower paste	A strong edible paste which can be rolled very finely. Is an ideal medium for making sugar flowers and can also used for some modelling work
Clear corn syrup	See 'liquid glucose'		
Cling film	Food wrapping film		
CMC	Carboxymethylcellulose, a synthetic and less expensive form of gum tragacanth. Often used as a thickening agent and as an edible glue	**Food net**	Protective mesh covering for foods
		Ganache	A mixture of chocolate and cream used for filling, piping, and covering cakes and petit fours (small sweets)
Cocoform	Trade name for modelling chocolate		
Collars	Royal icing run-out pieces which are attached to a cake top and extend beyond the cake edge	**Gift cake**	Small cake presented as a gift (guest cake)
		Gildesol	Edible gilding cream which can be used in conjunction with edible dusts, including metallic and lustre colours, to highlight the colour
Complementary colours	Colours opposite each other on the colour wheel		
		Gilding	See 'edible gilding'
Copyright	Exclusive protected ownership (e.g. of a design, product or publication)	**Glycerine**	Sweet, clear thick liquid often added to royal icing where a softer setting to flat icing is

required. Can also be used in baking and as an ingredient in piping chocolate and can be found in some paste food colours

Gum arabic — Fine white powder with many culinary uses. Can be mixed with water and used in cake decorating as an edible glue, in combination with gold and silver leaf, for example

Gum tragacanth — Fine, almost white powder, harvested from the Astragalus Gummifer tree, often used for thickening and strengthening. High quality and more expensive than CMC

Harmonious colours — A colour scheme using a mix of between three to six colours which are next to each other on the colour wheel

Icing sugar — Also known as confectioners' sugar, finer than granulated and caster sugar

Jam — Also known as jelly or conserve, can be used as a filling in cakes

Lacework — Small piped royal iced designs, without an outline, attached to the cake. Made as offset pieces

Liquid glucose — Also known as clear corn syrup, a simple sugar in the form of a thick opaque liquid. Frequently an ingredient in sugarpaste and modelling chocolate as it gives pliability

Marzipan — A mix of ground almonds, sugar and egg, marzipan is often commercially made and may contain other ingredients. A high quality marzipan will contain a high percentage of ground almonds. The paste is used for covering cakes, modelling and sweet and biscuit making.

MDF — Medium density fibre board, can be cut to size and used as a strong cake board

Modelling chocolate — Also known as Cocoform and plastic chocolate, a malleable paste made from a mix of chocolate and liquid glucose

Monochromatic — A colour scheme using various tints and shades of one colour

Monogram — Two or more initials intertwined

Oasis — Holding block for fresh or dried flowers. Available from florists, garden centres and some DIY stores

Offset pieces — Decorations which are prepared and finished and then attached or placed onto a cake

Pastillage — Very strong type of icing used for modelled structures and plaques. Can also be used to make pillars

Petal paste — See 'flower paste'

Pic — Small food grade holders specifically designed to be inserted into a cake to hold wired sugar flowers

Pillar — Decorative object designed to separate the tiers of a celebration cake

Piping bags — Conical shaped bags made from greaseproof paper, nylon or polythene, used to hold icings, creams, buttercreams etc., for piping. Can be used in conjunction with piping tubes

Piping tube — For use in the end of piping bags, also known as piping nozzles and tips.

Piping nozzle — See 'piping tube'

Plain flour — Also known as all purpose flour

Royal icing — A mix of egg white and icing sugar used for covering, piping and meringue making

Run-out — Royal iced piped outline filled with flood icing, normally prepared as offset pieces

Salmonella — A harmful bacteria which can cause food poisoning

Savoy tube — Large piping tube often used for piping buttercream as well as savoury items such as duchesse potatoes

Separator discs — Clear food grade plastic discs used as a protective layer to separate food from non-food grade items, e.g. for use between a cake and a non-edible decoration

Slating — Royal icing breaking off in thin layers when cut. A process caused when the icing used to cover a cake has not been consistent in recipe and the layers do not bond together properly

Smoothers — Flat oblong-shaped tools used to smooth the surface of marzipan, sugarpaste and similar coverings

Stacked design — A two or more tiered cake where the tiers are placed directly on top of each other

Stay soft — Soft malleable fixative used to secure floral and craft items. Available from florists and garden centre outlets

Sugarpaste — Soft roll-out icing, sometimes known as rolled fondant icing

Tempering — A process involving the heating and cooling of chocolate (or couverture) to specific temperatures allowing the different types of fats to blend with each other. Will give chocolate the gloss and 'snap' associated with a high quality chocolate when used

Top table — Table seating principal guests at a celebration

Trefoil — Clover leaf shaped

ACKNOWLEDGEMENTS

Many thanks go to Squires Kitchen, Orchard Products, Diamond Paste & Mould Co., Alister Thorpe and David Moore.

THANKS

So many people have helped in different ways, but I would particularly like to say a special thank you to Sarah Richardson, Jenny Stewart, Sue Hodges, Eddie Spence and Beverley Dutton whose help has been immeasurable. They have all helped to make writing this book a pleasure.

Especial thanks, too, to my sister, Jan, and my Dad for their loving support.

MANUFACTURERS AND DISTRIBUTORS

Stephen Benison
28 Rodwell Park
Trowbridge
Wiltshire
BA14 7LY
Tel: 01225 768649
Manufacturers of Link Twist cutter collection.

Diamond Paste and Mould Company
78b Battle Road
St. Leonards on Sea
East Sussex
TN37 7AG
Tel: 01424 432448
Specialists in rubber moulds and realistic veiners.

CelCakes & CelCrafts
Springfield House
Gate Helmsley
York
Yorkshire
Tel: 01759 371447
Suppliers of floral aids for sugarcraft and cold porcelain.

Guy, Paul & Co.
Unit B4
Foundry Way
Little End Road
Eaton Socon
Cambridgeshire
PE19 3JH
Tel: 01480 472545
Trade suppliers of tools and materials for the art of bakery,
sugarcraft and food decoration.

Holly Products
Holly Cottage
Hassall Green
Sandbach
Cheshire
CW11 4YA
Suppliers of moulds, embossers, patterns and tools via mail order.

Squires Group
Tel: +44 (0) 1252 711749
Web site: www.squires-group.co.uk
Online shop: www.squires-shop.com
Manufacturer of specialist sugars and food colourings.

SHOPS

Orchard Products
51 Hallyburton Road
Hove
East Sussex
BN3 7GP
Tel: 01273 419418
Manufacturers and suppliers of fine quality sugarcraft cutters
and tools. Shop and mail order.

Squires Kitchen Sugarcraft
(International School of Cake Decorating and Sugarcraft)
Squires House
3 Waverley Lane
Farnham
Surrey
GU9 8BB
Tel: 01252 711749
Web site: www.squires-group.co.uk
Online shop: www.squires-shop.com
Sugarcraft colours, tools, equipment, silver separators,
couverture, marzipans and sugarpastes. Shop, school and
mail order.

PUBLICATIONS

Merehurst (an imprint of Murdoch Books UK)
Ferry House
51-57 Lacy Road
Putney
London
SW15 1PR
Tel: 020 8355 1480
Publishers of many cake decorating and sugarcraft titles.

Squires Kitchen Magazine Publishing Ltd.
Alfred House
Hones Business Park
Farnham
Surrey
GU9 8BB
Tel: 01252 727572
Web site: www.squires-group.co.uk
Publishers of Cakes & Sugarcraft Magazine,
Wedding Cakes - A Design Source and Christmas Cakes,
Desserts & Sweets.